Freedom
IN DESIGN

New Directions in Foundation Paper Piecing

Mia Rozmyn

That Patchwork Place

Credits

Editor-in-Chief	Barbara Weiland
Technical Editor	Laura M. Reinstatler
Managing Editor	Greg Sharp
Copy Editor	Liz McGehee
Proofreader	Leslie Phillips
Illustrators	Lisa McKenney, Laurel Strand
Photographer	Brent Kane
Photographer's Assistant	Richard Lipshay
Design Director	Judy Petry
Cover and Text Designer	David Chrisman
Production Assistant	Claudia L'Heureux
Cover Calligraphy	Cindy Louie

Freedom in Design
New Directions in Foundation Paper Piecing
© 1995 by Mia Rozmyn
That Patchwork Place, Inc., PO Box 118, Bothell, WA 98041-0118 USA

Printed in Hong Kong
00 99 98 97 96   6 5 4 3 2

Library of Congress Cataloging-in Publication Data

Rozmyn, Mia,
    Freedom in design : new directions in foundation
paper piecing / by Mia Rozmyn.
        p. cm.
    ISBN 1-56477-102-4
    1. Patchwork—Patterns 2. Machine quilting.
3. Patchwork quilts. I Title.
TT835.R697 1995
    746.46—dc20   95-6592
                                          CIP

DEDICATION

I remember standing next to my mother while she painted.
She taught me umber,
sienna,
vermilion,
and cobalt.

She taught me that the tube of white should be the largest.
"You need lots of white to mix the other colors."

She taught me to see the different colors mixed together.
The blue in yellow,
the red in green.
Sienna in nearly everything.

"You use very little black,
But it ties the other colors together."

She taught me to see in color.

ACKNOWLEDGMENTS

Thanks and appreciation to:

Edward, my husband, who paid for all that silk and who puts up with an ironing board in the living room and scraps absolutely everywhere;

Geoff and Greg, who encourage me, give me ideas for quilts, tell me how beautiful they are, and pick up all my pins even when I won't come play Monopoly;

Diane Ross, who not only created "Otto," but also lit a fire under me to submit my proposal for this book. Without her encouragement, it would probably still be on the drawing board;

Julie Ketter, the real Otto Frog's "mom," for letting me put her friend in this book;

Elizabeth Hendricks and her friends Margaret Miller, Susan Wells Hall, Marty Kutz, and Nancy Lee Chong, who created the lovely "Butterfly's Ponytail Dreams" in their round robin;

Nancy Lee Chong again, my "Quilt Angel," who patiently and good humoredly listens to my oddball jokes and generously lends me "Arcturus Moons" whenever I need it;

Kathleen O'Hanlon, my first friend and student to actually complete a quilt, then win a prize for it! I'm very proud of her;

Teresa Posakony, for kindly allowing me to include Kathleen's quilt in this book. I know she missed it while it was gone;

Michel Jolivet, for lending me "Zion" whenever I need it, and for the lovely stained-glass window he made me. It gives me pleasure every time I see it;

Selena Bolotin, for making "Iris Moon" what it is—twice! Her patience, time, effort, and fabric choices are greatly appreciated;

Carol Olsen, for sharing her "Broken Hearts";

And to Emma, Sadie, Rhoda, Iowa, and Auntie, my real, for-sure quilt angels who directly or indirectly taught me everything about a needle and thread that I really needed to know.

Contents

PREFACE

The material in this book draws heavily from the established techniques available to all quilters. String piecing and polygons (many-sided shapes) have been used in patchwork almost since it began. Template and foundation-piecing methods have also long been part of the quiltmaking tradition. Many books document the use of freezer paper for these techniques, but I am indebted to one of my favorite quilters, teachers, and writers, Joen Wolfrom, for my first introduction to it. At the end of her "Landscapes and Illusions" class she pulled out a roll of freezer paper and showed us how to cut pieces, draw registration marks, and staystitch the edges. Although I had been using stay stitching and registration marks for years in garment construction, this was the first time I had seen them used in patchwork. Joen also suggested the pinning technique presented in this book.

I have always been able to design things I couldn't begin to piece. Although Joen only talked about her technique for a tantalizingly brief period, I think she opened a door to a piecing technique for which I had been searching.

That winter, I began using and developing the technique to suit myself. Many were the pitfalls I encountered! It was a little like exploring new terrain without knowing where the dangers lie.

To date, I've made over twenty-five quilts using the method of foundation freezer-paper piecing by machine. After friends began asking me to teach them the methods that evolved from this technique, I developed classes in piecing and design, which I now teach.

As I developed material for this book, other authors' work describing this method began appearing in various publications. Articles on the subject have been published in nearly every major quilting magazine.

Despite the material that has been written on freezer-paper piecing, I feel there is room for more. Quilters who have mastered the basic mechanics can construct their own original designs and place their seams wherever they wish. Gone are the limitations inherent in other methods. With this freedom to design, the only limit is the quilter's own imagination!

J

ABOUT THE QUILTS IN THIS BOOK

This is a process book. Use the techniques described for a variety of styles and design approaches. Although most of the quilts pictured in this book have a definite contemporary flair, the same techniques work for many traditional designs.

I have included plans for making seven quilts, each placed in the book according to their level of difficulty. If you prefer to design and make your own quilt, please read the section on "Developing Your Own Pattern" on pages 88–99. After reading this section, read carefully through the instructions given for each piecing method to fully understand the processes before starting on your own design.

For inspiration, see the photos of the quilts at the beginning of each section and in the Gallery of Quilts on pages 8–13. Patterns are not included for the gallery quilts because I didn't want the book to compete in size with the New York telephone directory!

HOW THIS BOOK IS ORGANIZED

The following pages include instructions that enable you to transform your designs into quilts. From a sketch, you will make a full-size cartoon (drawing of the quilt), then make a second drawing of the quilt on a single sheet of freezer paper. After cutting this freezer-paper pattern into individual pieces, you will iron them onto selected fabrics and prepare them for sewing your quilt.

The first technique introduced, simple piecing, shows how to construct a basic block, which illustrates the general curved-seam piecing process.

String and polygonal piecing follow, again illustrated with basic blocks. Designing with polygons and combining freezer-paper machine piecing with other piecing techniques, such as appliqué, come next. The book finishes with sections on developing your own designs and transforming a pieced top into a completed quilt.

FREEZER-PAPER MACHINE PIECING

Freezer-paper machine piecing includes two related techniques for sewing patchwork. The first technique, simple piecing, uses freezer-paper templates to shape and control the fabric as it is sewn together by machine. Freezer paper eliminates stretching and accurately marks the seam line, making curved piecing painless and taming even difficult fabrics, such as lamé and silk. Original designs can be created and duplicated. Basting is eliminated because the freezer paper is ironed to the fabric, holding it in place.

The second technique uses the freezer paper as a foundation. A piece of freezer paper, cut to a specific shape, serves as a pattern to which multiple pieces of fabric are sewn until the entire foundation is covered. Historically, foundation piecing was done on muslin or various types of paper. Crazy quilts are usually made using a form of foundation piecing.

This technique is for anyone who wants the speed of machine piecing combined with the freedom to put their seams anywhere they choose. It is for quilters who have explored more traditional piecing techniques and found them limiting; it is for traditional quilters who want to piece more challenging designs accurately; and it is for contemporary quilters who want to create original designs without fuss. A previous knowledge of other piecing techniques isn't necessary. Many students attending my classes who have never made a quilt before have turned out pieces as well crafted as any veteran quilter. It can also expand the horizons for more experienced needleworkers.

I'M GOING TO EAT YOU LITTLE FISHEYS

By Mia Rozmyn, 1993, Seattle, Washington, 49" x 66". The hand-dyed silk koi swim through kelp in gentle undersea eddies.

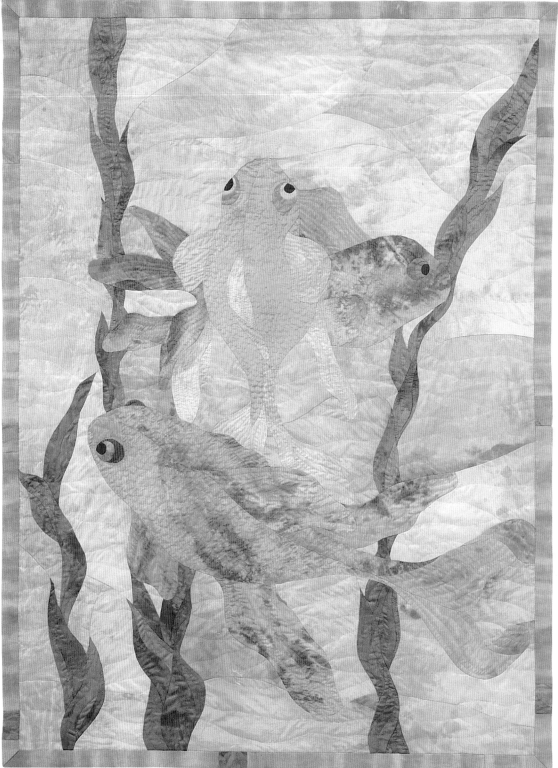

DRAGONFLY

*By Mia Rozmyn,
1994, Seattle,
Washington,
31" x 25". Layers
of small cotton
quilts work to-
gether to create an
illusion of depth
in this whimsical
soft sculpture.*

PUDDLE

*By Mia Rozmyn,
1993, Seattle,
Washington,
55" x 44".
Circular ripples in
a puddle on a
mossy brick
terrace reflect an
orange sunset.*

F O U R

R I N G S

By Mia Rozmyn, 1993,
Seattle, Washington,
37" x 37". A Dresden Plate,
a Mariner's Compass, a
New York Beauty, and a contemporary bird design
make up this sampler of string-pieced designs with
a border reminiscent of the Wedding Ring pattern.

TIBETAN
PANEL
COAT

*By Mia Rozmyn,
1992, Seattle,
Washington.
Natural, white,
and dyed silks
gleam on this
wearable art
based on the
FolkWear®
pattern #118.*

FOUR
STAR
QUILT

*By Mia Rozmyn,
1994, Seattle,
Washington,
37" x 37". Tradi-
tional New York
Beauty blocks in a
semicircular de-
sign are bordered
by overlapping
rings that draw
the eye round and
round again.*

NINE

SISTERS

*By Mia Rozmyn, 1994,
Seattle, Washington,
80" x 94". In hand-dyed silk,
the nine planets orbit around
a dying orange sun and the
darkness of space.*

BUTTERFLY'S PONYTAIL DREAMS

By Elizabeth Hendricks, Margaret Miller, Susan Wells Hall, Marty Kutz, and Nancy Lee Chong, 1994, Seattle, Washington, 62" x 80". The central sleeper with the string-pieced ponytail is surrounded by her couched dreams and a pieced border of polygons. Collection of Elizabeth Hendricks. Photography by Ken Wagner.

NESTING PLACE OF THE SHEN LUNG

By Mia Rozmyn, 1992, Seattle, Washington, 32" x 44". A modern offspring is hatched to a most traditional parent in this silk and cotton scrap quilt inspired by a fifteenth-century illustration.

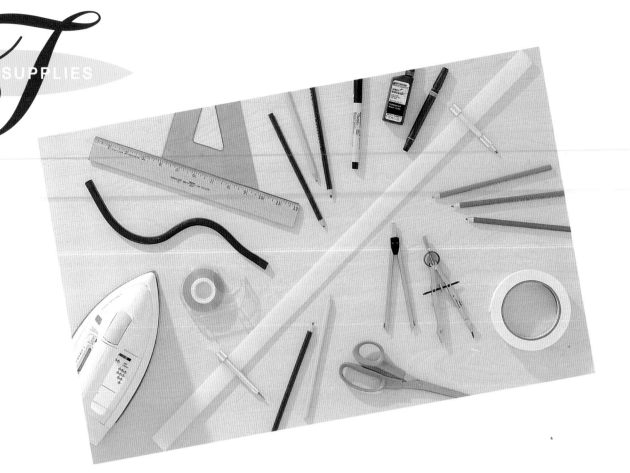

PAPER

For this process, you must first draw a full-sized line drawing of the quilt design, called a cartoon. Use any sturdy, white paper for the cartoon, then you can pin the pattern pieces to it. White paper allows you to see the lines on the cartoon better, making it easier to trace them. Butcher or bond paper is a sturdy, inexpensive paper available at drafting- and art-supply stores. It comes in 36"- and 48"- wide rolls.

After making the cartoon, make a second drawing of the design that you will cut up to use as a pattern. Every brand of freezer paper that I've used has worked quite well for the pattern. It is available in grocery stores and in some quilt shops. White freezer paper is translucent enough to allow dark lines to show through without being illuminated from behind. In some areas, only brown freezer paper is available. This works also, but you will need a light table or window to see the lines when tracing through it.

PEN AND INK

Make the lines on the cartoon dark enough to trace through freezer paper. Most dark ink pens and some soft lead pencils will work on butcher paper. I sketch my designs in pencil first, then trace over the seam lines in ink.

A number of permanent ink pens can be used to mark on the shiny side of the freezer paper. Felt-tip laundry markers, Sharpie® pens, and drafting pens with ink designed for film all work. Experiment to find the pen that works best on your paper types.

Felt-tip pens dry up very quickly on a large design. My preferences for drawing both the cartoon and the pattern are Mars-Staedtler® or Kohinoor® drafting pens with a size #4 tip. These pens cost more than ordinary felt-tip pens, but they are refillable and reliable. I fill them with ink made for drafting on film. The ink is very black. These pens must be cleaned after each use.

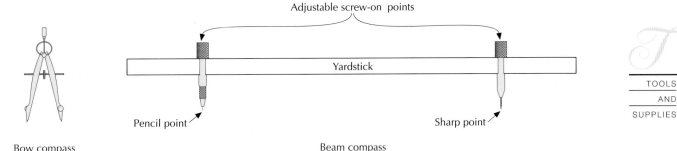

Adjustable screw-on points

Yardstick

Pencil point

Sharp point

Bow compass

Beam compass

TAPE

Tape the pattern and cartoon to the table or floor with masking tape. Drafters use a special tape (available from drafting-supply stores) that peels off easily without tearing the paper. To reinforce the corners of the cartoon, peel the tape off the table or floor when you have finished transferring the pattern, and wrap the tape around each corner. Then pin the cartoon to the wall through the reinforced corners. On large cartoons, reinforce the entire top edge with tape.

Tape

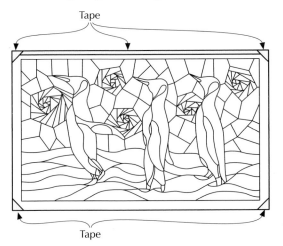

Tape

Use transparent tape (the kind you use for wrapping gifts) to join sections of butcher and freezer paper. Test your brand of tape on a scrap of paper before taping your pattern, then iron it. If it shrinks and peels off, try another brand.

Tape the matte side of the freezer paper, not the shiny side. If the tape is on the shiny side of the freezer paper, it can stick to the fabric when it is ironed down.

OTHER USEFUL DRAFTING EQUIPMENT

A wide variety of tools on the market make pattern drafting easier. Drafting-supply stores stock such helpful tools as T squares, straight edges, compasses, dividers, triangles in various angles, and lettering guides. Try the new flexible curves that are far superior to the old French curves for marking and copying irregular curves. Look for points that turn a yardstick or flat strip of wood into a large beam compass as illustrated above. These points can be moved along the yardstick to control the size of the circle.

Look in hardware stores for tools to make your tasks easier. A 36"- or 48"-long carpenter's aluminum straight edge is inexpensive and excellent for drawing long straight lines. A metal carpenter's tape is more accurate for measuring lengths longer than 36".

Look in your own supply stash for new ways to use old friends. For example, heavy white quilting thread works well as a guide for a straight line. (See "Squaring the Quilt" on pages 102–3.) Fortunately, the quilting industry is responding to quilters' needs, so many tools especially designed for quilters are available in quilt shops and catalogs.

SEWING SUPPLIES

Sewing Machine: It should be in good working order, capable of sewing a straight stitch with even tension.

Scissors: Use one pair for cutting paper, one for cutting fabric, and a short, pointed pair for clipping registration marks.

Needles: For machine piecing, use sizes 10/70 for silk and 12/80 for cotton.

Pins: Choose long, fine "quilters' pins" with plastic or glass heads for sewing and "T-pins" for squaring the quilt.

Seam Ripper: Useful for removing stitches easily.

Rotary Cutting Tools: A few techniques in this book require rotary cutting. For a complete list of supplies, see "Rotary-Cutting Basics" on page 36.

SIMPLE
PIECING

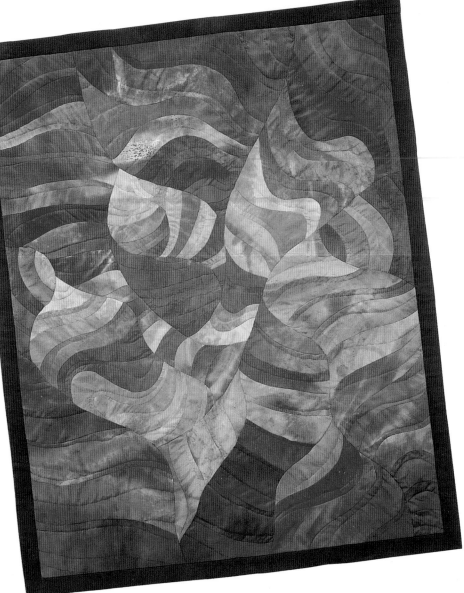

Zion by Mia Rozmyn, 1993, Seattle, Washington, 54" x 44". Purple and rust rocks flow around a bright center in this quilt inspired by the rocks at Zion National Park. Collection of Michel Jolivet.

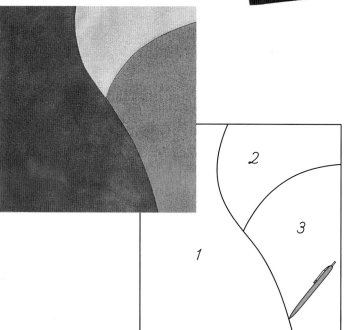

Simple piecing is a template technique for piecing curves in which there is one piece of fabric for each pattern piece. I am grateful to Joen Wolfrom for introducing me to the stay stitching, pinning, and registration-mark techniques explained in this section.

The photo at left shows the basic block. We'll walk through the entire method with this block first. After the basics are covered, the fine points will make much more sense.

MAKING
THE
CARTOON

A cartoon is a full-sized line drawing of the desired quilt design. It is the "road map" for the quilt. Never cut it into pieces. Draw a cartoon of the quilt on any sturdy, white paper. Draw it exactly the size you want the finished product to be. Draw seam lines where you want them; do not add seam allowances. Number the pieces and make any necessary notations about colors or fabric placement. Make the lines dark enough to show through another sheet of paper. A dark pencil or black ink pen works well.

MAKING THE PATTERN

Tape the cartoon to the table. Tape a piece of freezer paper of the same size over the cartoon with the shiny, plastic-coated side facing up. There is an important reason for this. You will iron the shiny side of the pattern to the wrong side of the fabric. If you trace the seam lines on the matte side of the paper, the image will be reversed. Trace only the seam lines onto the shiny side.

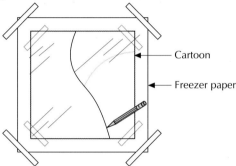

Cartoon

Freezer paper

Let ink dry before ironing the pattern to the fabric. If you are concerned about the ink transferring to the fabric, make a test sample first.

Carefully remove the tape and turn the pattern over. Write the pattern numbers on the matte side so that you can see them when you iron the freezer paper onto the fabric.

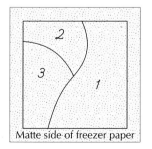

Matte side of freezer paper

DRAWING REGISTRATION MARKS

Registration marks are similar to the diamond-shaped markings on dress patterns. Seamstresses use them to align pattern pieces and they are particularly useful on curved seams.

Place registration marks according to your need, experience, and your tolerance for risk or error. If there are more marks on the seam line than you need, you can ignore them. But if they aren't there and you need them, you're in trouble. They don't take long to make, so be generous.

The general rule is, the tighter the curve, the more marks needed. On a smooth, shallow curve, such as the radius of a dinner plate, draw them every 3" to 4" apart. On a tight curve, such as the radius of a fifty-cent piece, draw them every 1/4" to 1/2".

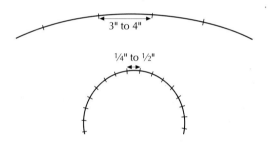

3" to 4"

1/4" to 1/2"

Always draw marks within 1/2" of the end of a seam or where two seams join.

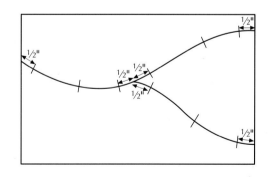

Fabric types also determine how many registration marks to make. I need fewer marks when sewing cotton than I do when working with silk, as it tends to be less stable.

Draw registration marks on the matte side of the freezer paper. For each mark, draw a 1/2"-long line across the seam line, being sure to make the marks perpendicular to the seam line.

Make additional notations, such as color or fabric choices, on the matte side now.

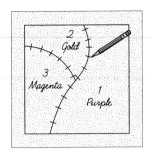

Cut the pattern pieces apart on the seam lines. Remember, the edge of the pieces represent the seam line so there is no seam allowance on the paper.

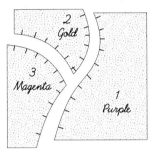

TRANSFERRING PATTERN NUMBERS AND STAYING ORGANIZED

The following tricks will help when you are transferring the pattern numbers to the matte side of the cartoon.

❧ Write pattern numbers on the shiny side of the freezer-paper pattern. Before you cut the pattern apart, turn it over and rewrite the numbers on the matte side. This takes a little longer, but you're less likely to misnumber something. If you have trouble seeing the numbers through the paper, try taping it to a window or light table.

❧ Number your pieces in an organized way, such as top to bottom, left to right.

❧ Number different sections of the design separately. For example, for a quilt similar to the example below, number the flowers, beginning with #1, number the pieces of the bells, beginning with #100, number pieces of the background, beginning with #200. Continue until all sections are numbered.

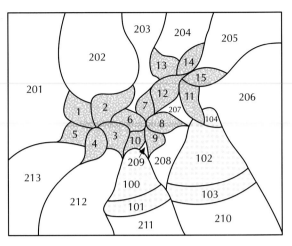

3 flowers, 2 bells, and background

Although this may result in gaps in your numbering system, it will help identify the pieces easily. Some of my quilts have over 300 pieces; when they are cut apart, they all look alike. An additional notation, such as "yellow flower," can also help.

❧ Orient all of the numbers in the same direction; don't turn the paper as you number it. Some pieces may be hard to reach on a large pattern, but it will help you orient the pieces once they are cut apart. Underline numbers that are easily confused like sixes and nines.

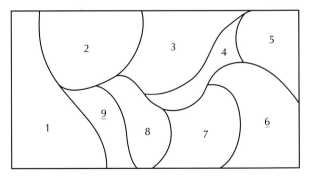

❧ Pin each pattern piece to the cartoon as you cut the pattern apart. This way, you can number any pieces you may have skipped. You are less likely to lose pieces and can remake any missing piece more easily.

❧ Remake a missing piece by laying adjoining freezer-paper pieces over a new piece of freezer paper and tracing the edges. Due to discrepancies that occur when drawing the cartoon, the missing piece's "hole" may be a slightly different shape than the original piece drawn on the cartoon.

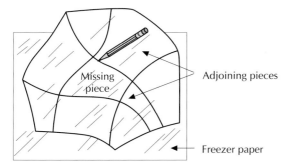

Missing piece

Adjoining pieces

Freezer paper

❧ Make sure that the registration marks and piece numbers appear on the matte side of the paper.

ATTACHING THE PATTERN PIECES TO THE FABRIC

There are few delights greater than piecing a nasty, misbehaving, difficult, but gorgeous fabric easily and having it look good! One of the strengths of freezer paper is that it "tames" difficult-to-handle fabrics.

Place each pattern piece shiny side down on the wrong side of the fabric, leaving at least 1/2" between pieces to allow for seam allowances.

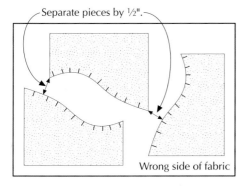

Separate pieces by 1/2".

Wrong side of fabric

Gently iron the *matte* side with a warm, dry iron set on wool for cotton and silk. Use a lower heat setting for fabrics that require it, but you may need to iron it a little longer. If the paper scorches, the iron is too hot, or you are ironing the piece too long. It only takes a few seconds to adhere the paper to the fabric.

Sometimes very sharp points or narrow pieces peel away from the fabric. To hold the paper to the fabric, run a machine-basting stitch right through both the paper and the fabric. Use a long stitch and don't backstitch so you can remove the stitching easily later.

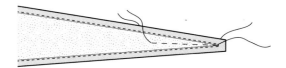

Transparent tape or a water-soluble glue stick also work to hold pattern pieces to the fabric.

Note: If you decide you want to change fabrics or if you forget to allow enough fabric for seam allowances and have already ironed the freezer paper to the fabric, peel the paper off and move it, then iron it again to the fabric. (I have never tested how many times you can do this before the paper stops sticking.)

If you iron the shiny side, as I have done occasionally, unplug your iron and let it cool thoroughly before peeling off the paper. Don't burn yourself. The plastic coating will not normally discolor or stick to your iron.

Cut out the pattern pieces, adding the seam allowances beyond the edge of the paper. (The 1/4"-wide seam allowance does not have to be extremely accurate.)

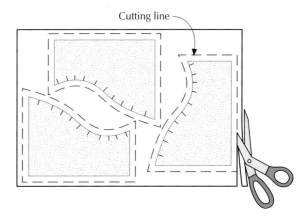

Cutting line

STAY STITCHING

Staystitch all the way around each piece to mark the seam line. Accurate stay stitching directly controls how flat your seams lie.

You have three thread-color options for stay stitching. Choose a different thread color from the thread you use to sew the seam. If you must remove stitches, you can easily tell which line of stitches to remove. Use a thread color that is in low contrast to the fabric so the stay stitching won't show badly if you inadvertently miss some.

Another option is to use a highly contrasting thread color so that you're more likely to see it without straining your eyes. A third choice is to use the same color thread that you plan to use for quilting and pretend that it's part of the design!

Use a long stitch length (six stitches to the inch is fine) and don't backstitch. If you need to remove the stay stitching later, it'll be easier.

For successful stay stitching, be sure to use the correct thread tension. If your machine puckers when you sew through a single layer of fabric, decrease the top tension. Experiment to achieve a stitch that allows the piece to lie flat. Remember, this stitching line is not the seam itself, so it is less important that the stitch be perfectly balanced than that the piece lies flat.

Stitch about one thread's width from the edge of the paper, staying within 1/8" of the paper's edge in the seam allowance.

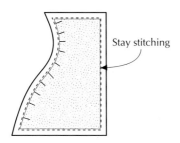

Stay stitching

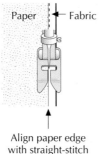

TIP Run the edge of the paper just along the inside of your straight-stitch presser foot. Experience and practice help a lot here. Don't worry about getting it perfect while you are doing the example block. When you've finished the block, you'll have a good feel for how accurate you need to be.

Paper ← Fabric

Align paper edge with straight-stitch presser foot.

FORGET THE REGISTRATION MARKS?

If you forget to draw the registration marks and have cut the pattern apart and ironed the pieces to the fabric, it's not too late to draw the marks. Fold back the seam allowance on one piece, slide it up to the neighboring piece, match the two sides, and draw the marks. This method, however, is slower and less accurate than marking the uncut pattern.

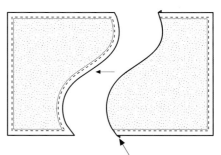

Fold back one seam allowance.

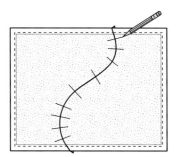

Draw registration marks.

If you drew the registration marks on the shiny side of the freezer paper and covered them with fabric, hold each piece up to a window or light table. If you can see them through the fabric, mark them on the matte side.

You may not be able to do this with cotton. If you are using simple piecing, peel the fabric loose just at the edges to see the marks, then clip the seam allowances at the marks, just up to the stay stitching as shown.

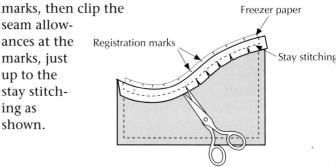

Freezer paper

Registration marks

Stay stitching

This technique works well for simple piecing but is not easy to do on string piecing. (See "String Piecing" on pages 35–41.)

CLIPPING THE REGISTRATION MARKS

Transfer the registration marks to the fabric by making a small clip in the seam allowance up to the stay stitching at each registration mark. Do not make additional clips now. *Never clip through the stay stitching.*

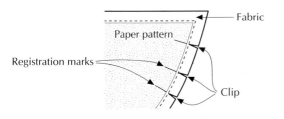

Note: Remove the freezer paper only before sewing a seam.

SEWING THE PIECES TOGETHER

Pinning. Work with only two pattern pieces at a time. (Pin the rest to the cartoon.) Select two pieces (pieces 2 and 3 of the sample block) that, when sewn together, join to make a continuous seam line for the next piece you will add. Place these two pieces right sides together and put a pin in the seam line to hold them together temporarily. Peel off the freezer paper.

Remove the temporary pin. Carefully align the stay stitching at the first registration mark. Poke a pin straight down through both layers just at the seam line. It should stick straight up out of the fabric. Check the alignment on the other side of the seam.

Slide another pin through both layers of fabric almost parallel to the fabric. Place it right next to the first pin. Make sure the first pin "stands" straight up and down; if it leans over,

the fabric layers have shifted. (If this happens, remove the second pin, realign the fabric to straighten the first pin and repin the second.) When it's pinned properly, remove the first pin. Pin each registration mark in the seam.

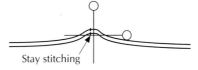

Clipping. Now clip to ease the fabric into the curve. Clip only the side that seems to stretch (this is the concave curve), not the "full" side (convex curve). If you wish to clip both sides, slip your scissors between the layers of fabric and clip them separately.

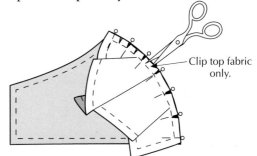

Do not clip through the stay stitching. Pin as much as you like between registration marks.

Always clip through the seam allowance of another seam before sewing over it. The whole piece lies flatter if seam allowances aren't caught in other seams. It is better to clip the seam allowances and fold them out of the way before you sew the seam than to try to clip them free later. Clip the seam allowance at right angles to the raw edges and just where the new seam will cross it.

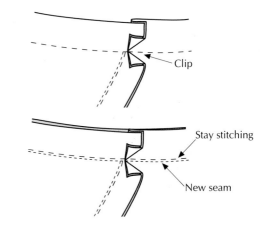

Sewing the seams. Thread tension is important when sewing seams. Balance the stitch as much as possible. If the seam still puckers, try changing the needle or thread types. If you have another machine, try using it instead. (I have an old machine that sews a beautiful seam for piecing and a somewhat less ancient machine that free-motion quilts. Someday, I want to invest in a *real* machine!)

Curved seams open up and expose the stitching more than straight seams do. Fabric is being eased and distorted and puts the thread under tension. This happens even when the seam allowances are pressed to one side.

To prevent the thread from showing, match the thread color to at least one of the fabrics being sewn together. Purists match the bobbin thread to the bottom fabric, and the needle thread to the top fabric. Some quilters compromise by choosing a neutral color, such as gray, that blends with both fabrics.

Shorten the stitch length to 10 to 12 stitches to the inch. This holds the seams together securely but allows the stitches to be ripped out if necessary.

Stitch beside the stay stitching, as close as possible to and just inside of it, as shown. Take care to stitch carefully and accurately for a seam that lies as flat as possible.

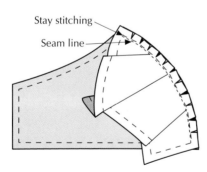

Stay stitching
Seam line

On curved seams, one fabric piece will be fuller than the other piece and will "bunch up" when pinned. Sew the seam with the full side on top to make sure you don't sew a tuck in the seam.

It is not necessary to pin and stitch an entire seam at one time. Sometimes working on a shorter section of the seam works better. This is particularly true of tightly curved seams and curves that change their direction.

Pin and sew as much of the seam as is com-

fortable to handle, ending where the curve begins to change direction, for example, from 1 to 2 in the diagram below. After pinning and stitching this section, remove the pins and move on to the next section, from 2 to 3, pinning, then stitching. Remove the pins from the completed section and complete the next section, from 3 to 4.

Do not sew across the stay stitching into the seam allowances. Start and end the seam at the corner where it meets the next seam. Backstitch at the ends of the seam.

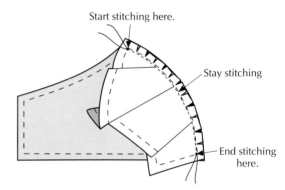

Start stitching here.
Stay stitching
End stitching here.

Remove the pins and open the two pieces. If the seam lies flat but the stay stitching shows, remove the stay stitching with a seam ripper. If the seam doesn't lie flat, remove the stitches, repin, and resew it. If necessary, check for stay stitching accuracy by laying the freezer-paper pieces back over the wrong side of each piece to find the error. After you have completed the first seam, press the seam allowances to one side. Repeat the steps above to sew the second seam.

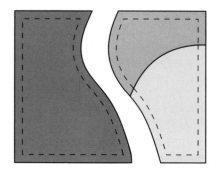

PRESSING SEAMS

Press the seam allowances toward the side that they tend to fall toward naturally. *Never press a seam open as you would in clothing construction.* The two seam allowances should always lie together so that the batting is hidden under the quilt top.

Where more than one seam ends at the same point, press the seam allowances in a spiral around the point.

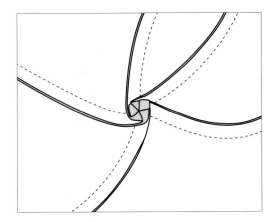

ASSEMBLING THE QUILT TOP

An unpieced quilt top resembles a jigsaw puzzle. Where do you start to put it back together? There are a few rules to follow.

Begin by sewing together two pieces that share a common seam. Check to see if the seam is shared by any other pieces.

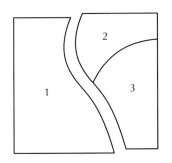

In the illustration above, pieces 2 and 3 fit neatly together. The seam that joins them is

not shared with any other pieces. Such seams are a good place to start.

Avoid constructing the quilt top by adding many small pieces to just one larger piece. Work across the quilt design, joining pairs of pieces to make larger pieces. Join these larger pieces into sections, then join sections to make the quilt top.

For a seam that cannot be completed with just two pieces, such as the one in the diagram below, sew the seam in parts, adding pieces as needed. To complete this example, sew from 1 to 2, then from 3 to 4, from 5 to 6, and then from 2 to 7.

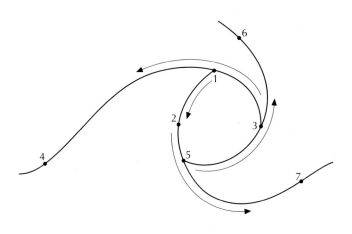

PROJECT:

LIGHT

HEARTS

20½" x 26"

This quilt design was inspired by a heart quilt that my friend Sue Lopez made as her first foundation machine-piecing project. Instead of repeating identical heart blocks, the blocks "flow," with the hearts varying in size and shape.

I made this version from hand-dyed silk scraps. Try substituting large-scale prints, soft "watercolor" fabrics, or gradated solids. Where two hearts overlap, try using colors that create a transparent look. Make jazzier versions, using high-contrast, vibrant prints.

Light Hearts by Mia Rozmyn, 1994, Seattle, Washington, 20½" x 26". Hand-dyed silk hearts quietly drift away in this small quilt.

MATERIALS   44"-WIDE FABRIC

¾ yd. for background

Assorted scraps for hearts

⅔ yd. for backing

22" x 28" rectangle of batting

¼ yd. or scraps for binding

18" x 44" rectangle of freezer
paper for pattern

MAKING THE PATTERN

1. Cut 2 pieces of freezer paper, each 18” x 22". Tape the long edges together, then trim to 22" x 28". Center the freezer paper, shiny side up, over the cartoon on the pullout pattern insert. Tape in place.

2. Prepare the freezer-paper pattern. (See "Making the Pattern" on page 17.) Cut apart the pattern pieces.

CUTTING THE FABRIC

1. Iron each freezer-paper pattern piece to the wrong side of the selected fabrics. (See "Attaching the Pattern Pieces to the Fabric" on page 19.)

2. Cut out the pieces, remembering to cut a ¼"-wide seam allowance beyond the edge of each paper pattern piece.

3. Staystitch around each piece. (See "Stay Stitching" on pages 19–20.)

4. Clip the registration marks. (See page 21.)

5. Pin the pattern pieces to the cartoon to see how they go together and to keep them organized.

ASSEMBLING THE QUILT TOP

1. Referring to "Sewing the Pieces Together" on pages 21–22, sew heart piece 5 to heart piece 4, and heart piece 24 to heart piece 23, matching registration marks. Press each seam as you sew it.

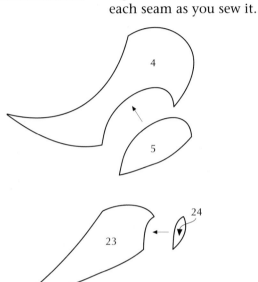

2. Work across the design, sewing each heart half into its background piece to make a "block." For example, sew heart half 2 into background piece 1, and heart halves 10 and 12 into background piece 11. Complete all of the blocks as shown below.

3. Sew blocks together into rows or bands. Sew the bands together.

4. Press the completed top.

COMPLETING THE QUILT

Refer to Section 7, "From Top to Finish," on pages 101–9.

1. Mark the quilt top with freehand hearts or as desired for quilting.

2. Layer the backing, batting, and quilt top. With the iron, press the layers together. Baste.

3. Quilt by hand or machine. I quilted "Light Hearts" with short wiggly lines that follow the flow of the design.

4. Square the quilt.

5. Bind the edges. (For double-fold binding, cut 3 strips, each 4" wide, across the width of the fabric from selvage to selvage.)

6. Label the quilt; sew on a hanging sleeve if desired. Share and enjoy!

Iris Moon *by Selena Bolotin, designed by Mia Rozmyn, 1994, Seattle, Washington, 26½" x 32". A warm yellow moon illuminates purple iris and charcoal rocks by a waterfall.*

PROJECT:

IRIS

MOON

32" x 26½"

Now that you have learned the basics about simple piecing, you are ready to put your new skills to work to make a more complex quilt. If you are not yet ready to design an original pattern (see Section 6, beginning on page 88), make the following quilt to build your skills further before going on to the next sections.

Before making "Iris Moon," review the general directions on pages 16–23.

The iris is one of my favorite flowers. One night, many years ago, I watched the moonlight move across our garden and pond. The memory of iris, moon, and water is the basis for this pattern.

A halo around the moon is common in Seattle, where there is a great deal of moisture in the air. My mother used to say that the number of stars you could count inside the ring around the moon was the number of clear days before it would rain again.

Selena Bolotin made this delightful quilt from my pattern, interpreting the design in her own fabrics.

MATERIALS   44"-WIDE FABRIC

¾ yd. or scraps for center panel

½ yd. for outer border

3" x 29" strip for inner border

¾ yd. for backing

28" x 34" rectangle of batting

¼ yd. for binding

18" x 54" rectangle of freezer paper for pattern

MAKING THE PATTERN

1. Cut 2 pieces of freezer paper, each 18" x 27". Tape the long edges together, then trim to 22" x 27". Center the freezer paper, shiny side up, over the cartoon on the pullout pattern insert. Tape in place.

2. Prepare the freezer-paper pattern. (See "Making the Pattern" on page 17.) Cut apart the pattern pieces.

CUTTING THE FABRIC

1. Iron each freezer-paper pattern piece to the wrong side of the selected fabric. (See "Attaching the Pattern Pieces to the Fabric" on page 19.)

2. Cut out the pieces, remembering to cut a ¼"-wide seam allowance beyond the edge of the paper pattern.

3. Staystitch around each piece. (See "Stay Stitching" on pages 19–20.)

4. Clip the registration marks.

5. Pin the pieces to the cartoon so that you can see how they go together and keep them organized.

Note: This pattern includes a few tight curves, pushing the limits of this method. If a curve becomes too difficult, consider appliquéing the seam instead.

ASSEMBLING

THE

QUILT

TOP

1. Assemble the quilt, following the numerical order given, or choose an assembly order of your own.

2. Section A: Sew pieces 1 and 3 to piece 2; add piece 4. Sew this unit to piece 5.

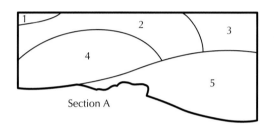

Section A

3. Section B: Sew pieces 12 and 24 to 6. Section C: Sew pieces 7 to 8, and 10 to 11, then sew both of these units to piece 9. Section D: Sew pieces 15 and 17 to piece 16.

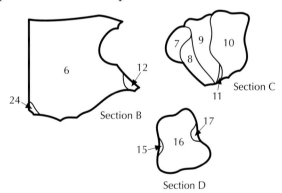

Section B

Section C

Section D

4. Section E: Sew piece 13 to 14, then add pieces 25 and 26. Section F: Sew piece 19 to piece 18, then add piece 20. Section G: Sew pieces 21, 23, 27, and 28 to piece 22; then add piece 29 to complete the unit.

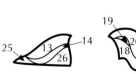

Section E

Section F

Section G

5. Section H: Sew pieces 30 and 47 to piece 34. Sew pieces 36 and 48 to piece 35. Sew piece 38 to piece 49, then add piece 37. To this unit, sew piece 50, then add piece 39. Sew these three units together to make the section.

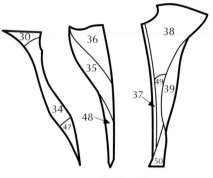

Section H

6. Section I: Sew pieces 43 and 46 to piece 44, then add piece 45 to the top of the unit. Section J: Sew piece 51 to piece 52.

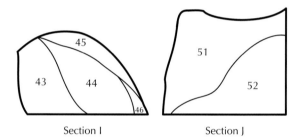

Section I

Section J

7. Sew the compound pieces together into larger sections: Sew Section B to Section E. Sew Section F to Section G.

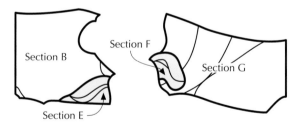

Section B

Section F

Section G

Section E

8. Sew Sections BE and GF to Section C.

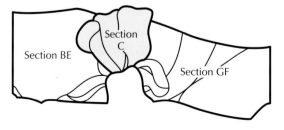

Section BE

Section C

Section GF

9. Sew Section A to the section assembled in step 8, sewing the curves around the petals in separate sections as indicated by arrows. (See "Sewing the Seams" on page 22.)

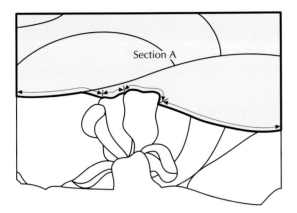

10. Sew Section H to the section made in step 9. Omit Section D; it will be added later. In the following order, add pieces 33, 32, 31, and 40. (See Tip at right.)

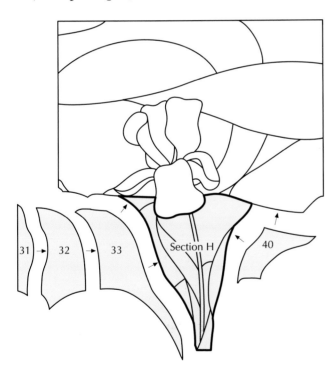

TIP When adding piece 40 to pieces 38 and 29, sew the set-in seam more easily by removing 1¼" of stitching from the seam along piece 38 where it joins piece 29.

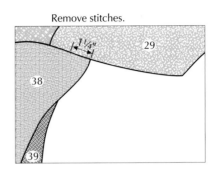

Remove stitches.

Sew the left side of piece 40 to unit 38/39.

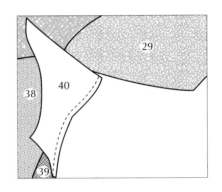

Pin and resew the seam along piece 38, following the direction of the arrow. Continue sewing the seam, sewing piece 40 to piece 29.

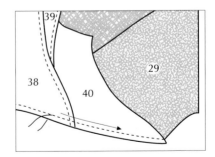

11. Sew section I in place, then add piece 42. Sew piece 41 to unit 40/29, then add Section J.

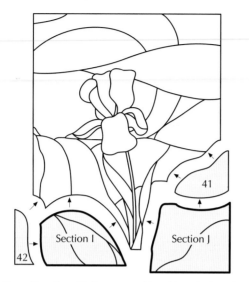

12. Sew Section D last, appliquéing it in place if you do not wish to piece it. (See "Combining Foundation Piecing with Appliqué" on pages 77–78.)

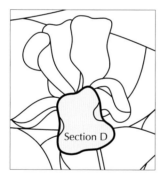

13. Press the completed top.

ADDING

THE

BORDERS

1. Square the quilt top. (See "Squaring the Quilt" on pages 102–3.

2. Cut 4 strips, each 3/4" wide, from inner border fabric. Measure through the center of the quilt from the top to the bottom edges. Cut 2 strips to this measurement and sew a strip to each side of the quilt.

3. Measure through the center of the quilt from side to side, including the borders you just added. Cut the remaining strips to this measurement and sew a strip to the top and bottom of the quilt.

4. Measure the length of the quilt through the center, add 4¼", then cut 2 outer border strips, each 4½" wide, to this length. Place 1 strip at the top of the quilt, keeping the left edge even with the left side of the quilt, and leaving the extra length at the right side of the quilt, as shown. Sew to within 1" from the right edge of the quilt top. Press seam allowances to one side.

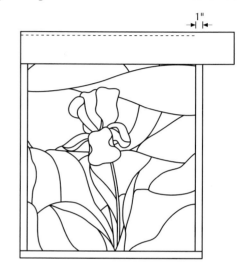

5. Measure the quilt through the center, including the newly added border, then cut 2 outer border strips, each 4¼" wide, to this length. Pin one strip to the left side of the quilt top, keeping the lower end even with the edge of the quilt. Stitch. Press seam to one side.

6. Pin the lower border to the bottom of the quilt top; stitch, then press. Pin the remaining side border to the right side of the quilt; stitch, then press seam to one side.

7. Sew the top border to the right border by completing the seam as shown. Press.

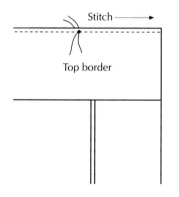

Stitch ⟶

Top border

COMPLETING

THE

QUILT

Refer to Section 7, "From Top to Finish," on pages 101–9.

1. Mark the quilt as desired for quilting.

2. Layer the backing, batting, and quilt top. Baste.

3. Quilt by hand or machine.

4. Square the quilt.

5. Bind the edges.

6. Label the quilt; sew on a hanging sleeve if desired. Share and enjoy!

Bon Odori by Mia Rozmyn, 1992, Seattle, Washington, 65" x 85". Hand-dyed silk rainbows flutter before a dark sky.

STRING

PIECING

 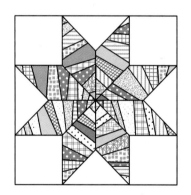

String-Pieced Star
with Angled Seams

String piecing has a long history in traditional quilting. The term refers to piecing long narrow strips of fabric together to make a larger piece, which is then sewn to other large pieces. The main difference between strip and string piecing is that in strip piecing the seams are always parallel, and in string piecing the strips are frequently wedge shaped. Dresden Plate, Double Wedding Ring, Spider Web, Mariner's Compass, New York Beauty, and Pickle Dish are all patterns that can be constructed using the string-piecing technique.

In string piecing, simple pieces are covered with small wedge-shaped strips called "strings" and then assembled to make larger sections or blocks. This section focuses on the string-piecing process and some of its design features. To assemble string-pieced units into a quilt top, refer to Section 1, "Simple Piecing," on pages 16–23 for piece assembly.

Strips with parallel edges may be used as strings. The sewn shape is controlled by seam placement.

ROTARY-

CUTTING

BASICS

Cut shapes such as strings, strips, squares, bricks, borders, and binding easily and accurately, using rotary-cutting techniques. Rotary cutting is fastest when you cut up yardage into many identical shapes. For most purposes, cut strings and strips across the width of the fabric from selvage to selvage. Cut borders across the width of the fabric or cut them lengthwise for long, seamless strips.

For rotary cutting, you need a rotary cutter, straight-edge ruler, Bias Square®, and cutting mat. Rotary cutters are available in three different blade sizes. For all-purpose cutting, choose a cutter with a 1¾"- diameter blade.

As a cutting guide, choose a 3" x 22" or 6" x 24" see-through, ⅛"-thick acrylic ruler, with accurate lines. For squaring fabric and cutting segments, use a 6" or 8" Bias Square.

Self-healing cutting mats are necessary to protect both the work surface and the cutting blade and come with or without grids. The marked grids are helpful when lining up the cutting edge to make accurate 45°- or 90°-angle cuts.

The first step in rotary cutting is to square the end of the fabric. This ensures a straight strip. If the end of the folded fabric isn't square, the resulting strip will be shaped like a V or W.

1. Fold the prewashed, pressed fabric in half lengthwise, aligning the selvages. Smooth the fabric out flat to the right, with the fold toward you and the raw edges on the cutting mat. (Reverse if left-handed.)

2. To make sure the cut will be at a right angle to the fold, place the edge of a Bias Square along the fold. Lay the cutting guide over the raw edges of the fabric, against the Bias Square and perpendicular to the fold. Make sure the entire raw edge of the fabric extends under the ruler.

3. Remove the Bias Square and, pressing straight down on the cutting guide to hold it firmly, make the cut by pushing the rotary cutter away from you, along the edge of the ruler.

4. Lay the cutting guide over the cut edge of the fabric, with the edge of the fabric under the line on the ruler corresponding to the correct strip width. Cut along the edge. For example, to cut an accurate 2"-wide strip, align the edge of the fabric under

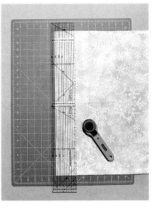

the 2" line on the cutting guide. Be as accurate as possible to ensure your strips are even and straight.

5. After you cut the strip, square the ends of the strip by cutting off the selvages. Lay the strip horizontally on the cutting mat and place the cutting guide's edge along one of the long cut edges of the strip. Move the guide along the strip until the ends of the strip lie under the correct line and make the second cut.

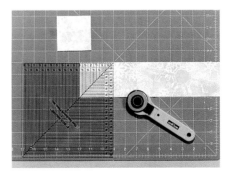

BEGINNING THE PROCESS

For our example, return to the basic block used in Section 1 on page 16. Instead of covering each pattern piece with one fabric, we will cover them with strings.

Use the following key for distinguishing the matte and shiny side of freezer paper.

Shiny or coated side of freezer paper

Matte or uncoated side of freezer paper

Make a pattern of the block, using freezer paper the same way you made the pattern in Section 1 on page 17. On the matte side, draw the registration marks and pattern numbers, then draw arrows indicating the orientation of the strings. These arrows aren't mandatory, but they act as a reminder when the pattern pieces are cut apart.

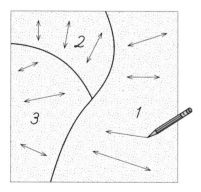

Matte side of freezer paper

Cut the pattern pieces apart. Now you are ready to begin covering each piece with strings.

APPLYING THE STRINGS

1. Cut fabric strips. At the ironing board, place the wrong side of the first fabric strip at the tip of the pattern piece so that enough fabric is sticking out for a seam allowance. (Remember, the edge of the paper pattern piece is the seam line so you must add seam allowances.) Iron the pattern to the fabric. This is the starter strip. From now on, follow a repetitive pattern of "sew and flip."

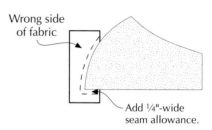

Wrong side of fabric

Add ¼"-wide seam allowance.

2. Place the second strip of fabric on top of the first, right sides together. Angle the strip, if necessary, so that it will lie across the pattern correctly when flipped.

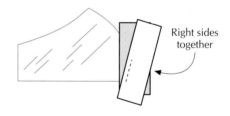

Right sides together

Note: Make sure that the strip sticks out far enough above and below the pattern to allow a ¼"-wide seam allowance beyond the paper when the strip is flipped over.

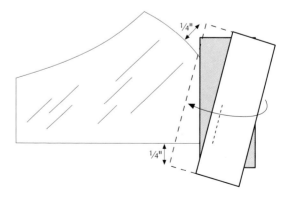

¼"

¼"

3. Sew a ¼"-wide seam from the edge of the second strip, through all three layers.

4. Trim any extra seam allowance from the first strip and flip the second strip over. Press in place.

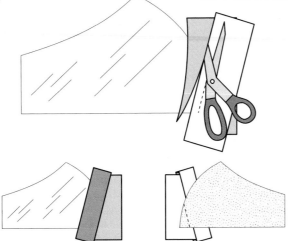

5. Repeat steps 2 and 3 until the entire pattern piece is covered. Trim away excess fabric beyond the ¼"-wide seam allowance around the pattern piece.

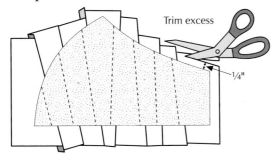

Trim excess

¼"

6. String-piece the remaining pattern pieces, staystitch around them, then clip registration marks. (See "Stay Stitching" on pages 19–20.) Remove the paper *just* before sewing pieces together, tearing it carefully at the stitching lines to remove it strip by strip. Assemble the string-pieced units to make the block, following the instructions for simple piecing on pages 16–23.

Now that you understand the basics of string piecing, let's look at the fine points!

MAKING THE CARTOON AND PATTERN

Although the cartoon and pattern are made essentially the same way in string piecing as they are in simple piecing, the pattern need not be made of freezer paper. Butcher or bond paper is easier to remove after stitching, and you can save drafting time by using a photocopy machine to make many copies of a pattern. (See "Photocopying" on page 95.) Copying a pattern directly rather than tracing it is ideal for blocks or repetitive designs, such as Double Wedding Ring or Pickle Dish. Remember, however, that the end strings will not stick to the bond paper as they do to freezer paper. Consider using pins, glue, or basting to keep the end strings in place while you sew the strings and staystitch around the pattern.

Try using Stitch-n-Tear® or other removable interfacings for pattern pieces. Stitch-n-Tear is slightly rough, so the fabric tends to cling to it. For large pattern pieces, sew pieces of Stitch-n-Tear together by lapping one edge over another and straight-stitching through both layers.

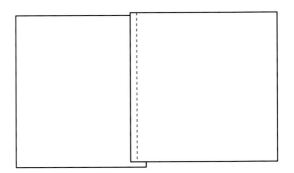

It's not necessary to remove Stitch-n-Tear after string piecing, but it can be torn out if you want a softer quilt.

When you mark arrows on the matte side of the pattern indicating the orientation of the strings, make them as minimal or hastily drawn as you wish for your own general reference. However, if you want the seams of your strings to line up between pieces, draw them on the pattern before you cut it apart. This will

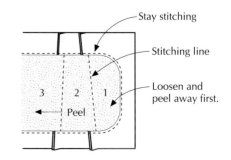

require carefully drafting seam lines for every string you intend to place. The second string-pieced example on page 41 uses this method.

If you cut the strings so that the edges are not parallel and sew all the narrow ends close together, the strings tend to spiral around a central point, forming a fan when sewn to the foundation fabric. To counteract this fan effect, alternate narrow and wide ends when sewing them to the foundation.

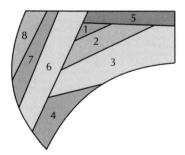

It's not necessary for the strings to extend across the pattern from one seam allowance to the other. Sew a few to an interior area of the pattern, then sew other strings across the exposed ends to cover them. In the illustrations below, the strings are numbered in the order that they are applied.

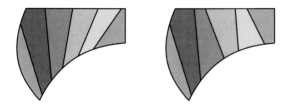

You also don't have to start at one end of a pattern piece when applying the strings. Begin at an interior point and add pieces, working toward the outside of the pattern piece.

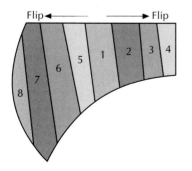

DETERMINING STRING WIDTH & SETTING STITCH LENGTH

Before you begin piecing, cut the strings and adjust the stitch length on your machine. As the designer, you decide the width to cut the strings. To allow for 1/4"-wide seam allowances, cut the strings at least 1/2" wider than the widest part of the area the string will cover and at least 1/2" longer than the area to be covered.

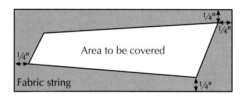

To cut strings quickly, rotary cut them as strips as shown on page 36. This is much quicker than trying to cut wedge-shaped strings that fit. Because the edges are not on the bias, they're not as likely to stretch.

Set the stitch length to at least 12 stitches to the inch or a 2mm length. When stitching, the needle creates a line of perforations that allows you to remove the paper easily later. Tearing the paper away, however, puts tension on the thread and can damage the seam. To help support the seam, use good-quality thread and shorten the stitch length as much as you like, even to 20 stitches to the inch.

Remove the paper by gently pulling it away from the string that was first applied to the pattern, then remove the paper from the adjacent string, continuing across the pattern until all paper is removed. Removing the paper from the first piece sewn to the pattern helps to keep the seam allowances from fraying.

REPAIRING A SHORT STRING

If you've applied a string and flipped it over only to find that it wasn't long enough, you have several possible remedies.

The best solution, but also the most difficult one, is to rip out the entire seam and replace it with a string of the correct length. It's easy to damage your pattern piece doing this, but you can repair it with tape.

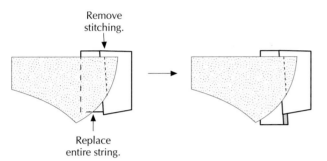

Remove stitching.

Replace entire string.

Another method is to remove just enough of the seam so you can sew an extension onto the string and then sew it back down again.

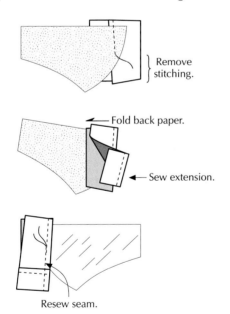

Remove stitching.

Fold back paper.

Sew extension.

Resew seam.

The least desirable solution is to sew an extension to the short string from the right side,

through the paper. Begin and end stitching ¼" from the edges of the string. Turn the side seam allowances under and appliqué the sides of the string extension to the adjacent strings. I've had to do this to repair a split in a silk string long after the strings were all applied. While this method extends or repairs the string, it takes a long time and it is difficult to appliqué the sides so that they lie smoothly.

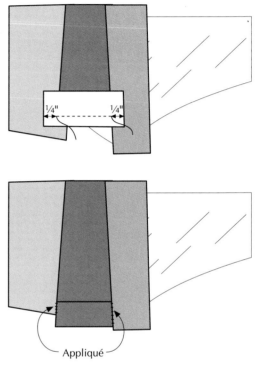

¼"   ¼"

Appliqué

STAY STITCHING

If you use a foundation that must be removed, staystitch around the edges, clip registration marks, then tear the paper away before you sew the pieces together. This helps when easing the curved seams. You may skip the stay stitching if your foundation won't be removed or if your seams are all straight lines. (See "Polygonal Piecing" on pages 48–53.)

Note: Cut the pattern apart on the curved seam lines, *not* the strings' sew-and-flip lines.

When sewing, keep the matte side of the freezer-paper pattern on top. Place the new strip and the previously sewn strip with right sides together on the bottom, against the shiny side of the paper. Sew directly on the seam lines drawn on the paper pattern. String-19

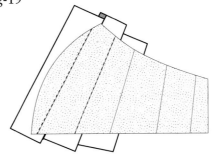

Sew on marked lines.

Because the strip is straight and extends beyond the paper, you can tell if it is lined up with the seam line.

MAKING A BLOCK WITH ALIGNED STRINGS

String piecing is most effective when combined with optical illusions. Achieve this by carefully choosing colors and laying out the strings so that each string aligns with the strings on adjoining pieces.

The illustration below shows each piece's strings sewn so that they align when the pieces are sewn together.

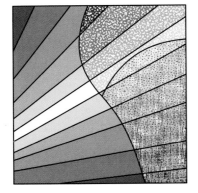

To do this, draw each string's sew-and-flip line on the paper pattern before you cut it apart and sew the strings. Use a divider or a drafting compass to evenly space lines and use a straight edge to draw them.

Note: A divider is an adjustable drafting tool used to mark equally spaced points.

PROJECT: TEA GARDEN

35" x 30"

The "strings" in this pattern are the rows of bricks, cut and sewn together using rotary-cutting techniques. Apply the bricks to the pattern piece using the same sew-and-flip technique discussed on pages 37–38.

Transparency, blending, and sleight of hand make this quilt design work. The contrast of value and hue when two fabrics or shapes meet contributes to the effect of transparency. Continuing the brick pattern across the circles, combined with the overall mottling of the fabric, allows the textures to blend, unifying the quilt. Where the seams defining the edges of the circles end, the circles seem to blend into each other, disappearing in places and creating a sense of magic or mystery.

When I designed this quilt, I focused on the circles and arcs, adding the bricks for texture and ease of construction. To make the incomplete circles, it was necessary to end the circles' seam lines where they intersect the straight seams of the bricks.

For my quilt, I used scraps of the hand-dyed silks that I love so much. Consider trying the watercolor techniques described in Deirdre Amsden's *Colourwash Quilts* or Pat Magaret and Donna Slusser's *Watercolor Quilts* (both from That Patchwork Place). Or, you may want to use some of the gradated fabrics now available.

Tea Garden by Mia Rozmyn, 1994, Seattle, Washington, 36" x 30". Overlapping circles in dreamy spring colors are the base for intensive quilting in a design taken from traditional Japanese textile motifs.

½ yd. (total) assorted blues

½ yd. (total) assorted pinks

½ yd. (total) assorted yellows

½ yd. (total) assorted greens

¾ yd. for backing

32" x 42" rectangle of batting

¾ yd. for binding

18" x 60" rectangle of
freezer paper for pattern

MAKING THE PATTERN

1. The pre-gridded image for "Tea Garden" appears on page 110. Referring to "Using a Grid" on pages 95–96, make a cartoon measuring 36" x 30".

2. To make the pattern, cut 2 pieces of freezer paper, each 18" x 30". Tape the long edges together, then trim to 36" x 30". Center the freezer paper, shiny side up, over the cartoon and tape in place. (See "Making the Pattern" on page 17.)

3. Trace the bold seam lines that outline the pieces. These lines indicate where the pieces will be sewn together into larger sections. When sewing the pattern pieces together, use the narrow seam lines that form the bricks as registration marks for positioning. Mark as many of these brick seam lines on the paper pattern as you need to line up the pieces.

4. Remove the tape. Turn the pattern over. On the matte side, mark the pattern numbers and draw the narrow brick lines. Draw additional registration marks on the curves as needed.

5. Cut the pattern apart on the heavy seam lines. Do not cut on the narrow (brick) lines. Pin the pieces to the cartoon to keep organized.

MAKING

THE

ROWS OF

BRICKS

1. Cut the fabric for the bricks into 2¹/₂"-wide strips, then cut across these strips at 3¹/₂" intervals to make 2¹/₂" x 3¹/₂" bricks. Arrange bricks into stacks of similar colors.

2. Remove the pattern pieces pinned to the cartoon and set aside. Pin the fabric bricks to the cartoon to audition them. Move them around until you like their placement. For the bricks made up of more than one fabric, fold them to roughly resemble their final shape.

Note: Define the general layout of colors now. Remember to emphasize the curves, which will appear as circles or parts of circles, by choosing colors in high contrast for opposite sides of the curved seams. Keep the bricks inside any one curve in low contrast to each other. Blend the colors where one area of the quilt flows into another.

3. Working with one pattern piece at a time, sew the bricks together in rows first across the pattern piece. Start with the top row and work down the piece. For example, consider piece 2 in the illustration above right. The first row at the top requires 3 bricks, the second row requires 4 bricks, the third row requires 3 bricks, and the bottom row requires 2 bricks. Use whole bricks on the ends of the rows; the extra will be trimmed off later. Sew rows of bricks together with ¹/₄"-wide seams. For each row, press the seam allowances in the same direction.

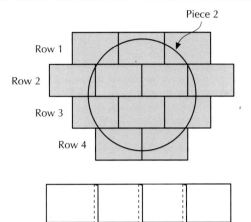

4. To prepare the first row for string piecing, lay the shiny side of the pattern piece over the wrong side of the correct row. Line up the seams, then press the pattern piece in place.

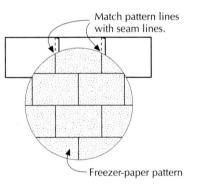

5. Lay the second row, right sides together, on top of the first row, lining up the bricks' seam lines with the lines drawn on the pattern. Sew the second row in place. Flip it over and press in place. Continue adding rows until the piece is covered.

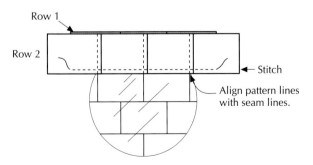

6. Staystitch around the edges of the piece. Trim away extra fabric, leaving a 1/4"-wide seam allowance, and clip the registration marks. Pin the pieces to the cartoon. Repeat steps 3–6 until each piece is covered.

ASSEMBLING

THE

QUILT TOP

PATTERN

1. Once all pattern pieces are covered, follow the directions for simple piecing on pages 16–23. Sew the pattern pieces together in the following order or in the manner easiest for you. As each piece is about to be sewn, remove the pattern from the back. Press the seam allowances to one side after each seam is sewn.

2. Aligning the edges of the bricks, sew piece 3 to piece 4 and piece 5 to piece 6. Sew piece 9 to piece 10, piece 11 to piece 12, and piece 16 to piece 17.

3. Sew piece 18 to piece 22, piece 20 to piece 21, piece 23 to piece 26, and piece 24 to piece 25.

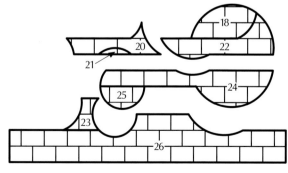

4. Sew the compound pieces together into larger sections. Sew piece 1 to unit 5/6, then add unit 3/4. Add piece 7, then piece 2.

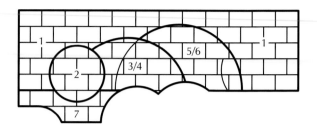

5. To the section made in step 4, sew unit 11/12. Add piece 8, then unit 9/10 and 16/17.

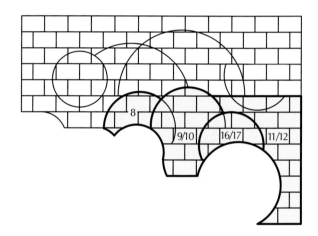

6. Sew unit 24/25 to unit 23/26. Add unit 20/21, then unit 18/22.

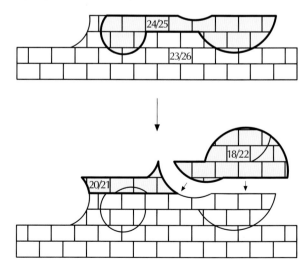

7. Sew the two large sections made in steps 2–6 together. Add piece 15, then piece 14. Inset pieces 13 and 19.

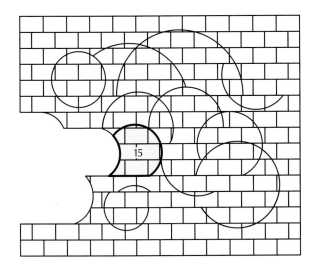

8. Press and square the completed top. (See pages 102–3.)

COMPLETING THE QUILT

Refer to Section 7, "From Top to Finish," on pages 101–9.

1. Mark the quilt as desired for quilting. I used flower patterns throughout the quilt.

2. Layer the backing, batting, and quilt top. Baste.

3. Quilt by hand or machine.

4. Square the quilt.

5. Bind the edges. I cut 5"-wide strips for the binding on my quilt to make a 1"-wide double-fold binding.

6. Label the quilt. Sew on a hanging sleeve if desired. Share and enjoy!

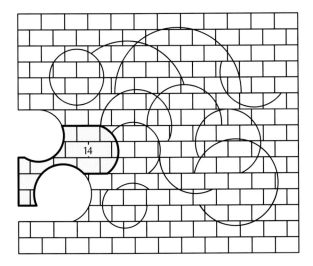

Broken Hearts
*by Carol Olsen,
1992, Bainbridge
Island, Washing-
ton, 38" x 38". Red
and orange frac-
tured hearts are set
off by a vivid
checkered border.*

POLYGONAL
PIECING

What is a polygon? Squares, triangles, dia-
monds, and other many-sided shapes are all
polygons. This chapter introduces a new approach to working with these old friends in an
easy way that traditional quilting's polygonal
shapes do not allow.

Polygonal design gives the quilter more control in placing color and line than string piecing, without losing the speed of piecing
straight-line seams.

Polygonal piecing frees the quilter from the
strong linear quality and parallel shading of
string piecing. You can achieve a faceted, jewel-
like image by juxtaposing similar hues and values. This section broadens the sew-and-flip
method presented for string piecing to include
any polygonal shape (except those with angles
greater than 180°). Once you learn an easy way
to piece polygons, you can explore designing
with them in the next chapter.

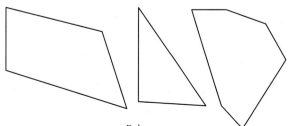

Polygons

Consider the original block design on page 16. In the photo below left, I have broken up the three original pattern pieces into many random polygons.

For polygonal piecing, I used many short, straight seams to approximate the curves of the original block's seams. The following instructions discuss cutting the pattern apart into chains of polygons, covering them with fabric using the sew-and-flip method, then joining the chains to make the block. Instead of numbering the pieces as you did in the original three-piece block, assign numbers or letters to identify the chains. I chose the colors in the polygonal pieced block to resemble the color areas in the original block. This shows more clearly the possibilities and similarities of the effects of the two methods.

TRACING

THE

PATTERN

Place the freezer paper, shiny side up, on the cartoon. Draw the seam lines on the shiny side of the freezer paper, then retrace them on the matte side. If you trace the seam lines directly onto the matte side, the image will be reversed when you sew the fabric to the paper. If you have a light table or draw the pattern at a window, you can reverse the cartoon and trace onto the matte side directly.

Shiny or coated side of freezer paper

Matte or uncoated side of freezer paper

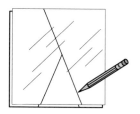

Drawing registration marks on the seam lines is not necessary when drawing the pattern, since the seams are all straight. Highlight the seams outlining the chains of polygons, then number them on the matte side.

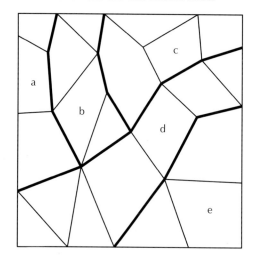

SEPARATING

THE

PATTERN

INTO

CHAINS

A chain is a row or area that can be covered with fabric using the sew-and-flip method, then sewn as a unit to other chains to make the quilt top. Any pattern can be separated into chains in a number of different ways.

When deciding where to cut chains apart, think of how you would link polygons by overlapping them. Keeping areas of color together in chains is not important, as some chain edges cross through color areas. The illustration below shows the piecing order of the polygons in the chain. This piecing order reflects the way the polygons overlap each other without requiring set-in seams. Each polygon leads to the next polygon like stepping stones in a pathway.

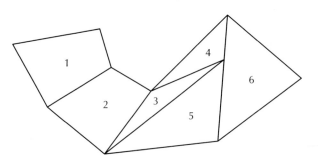

Sewing together many short, easy chains is better than making fewer long, difficult ones. Try to avoid Y seams; they are a bit tricky. A Y seam is one in which three seams join at one point. If it is impossible to avoid a Y seam, see "Piecing a Y seam" on pages 51–52.

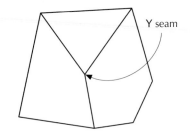

Y seam

1. To sew a polygonal block, first cut the pattern apart into chains. Separate the example block this way:

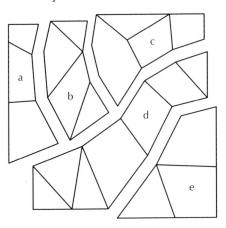

2. Beginning with chain 5, for example, place the wrong side of a piece of fabric against the first polygon in the chain. Make sure the fabric piece is big enough to cover the polygon and still allow at least a ¼"-wide seam allowance around the edges of the polygon.

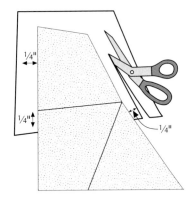

3. Iron the pattern onto the wrong side of the fabric.

4. Cut another piece of fabric to cover the next polygon. When pinning, place a pin or two along the stitching line of each seam and test flip the fabric before actually sewing the seam. This will save ripping out countless stitches. If you find that too many pieces need adjusting when you pin and flip, cut your fabric pieces a little more generously.

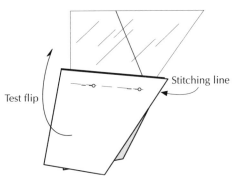

Test flip

Stitching line

5. If the fabric covers the polygon sufficiently, sew the seam, then backstitch. Do not sew beyond the edge of the paper. Trim seam allowances if necessary.

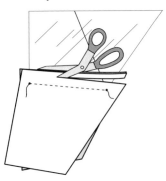

6. Clip perpendicular to the seam allowance you have just sewn at the point where it meets the edge of the paper. This technique allows you to avoid catching these seam allowances in intersecting seams later.

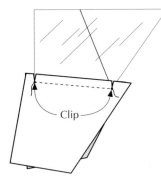

Clip

7. Flip the polygon over and iron it in place.

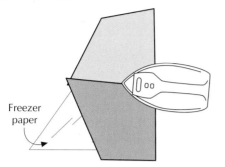

Freezer paper

8. Cover the rest of the first chain. Continue covering the remaining chains in this way.

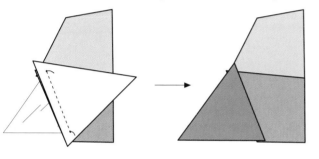

PIECING

A *Y* SEAM

There are two ways to deal with a Y seam.

Method 1

1. Separate the chain into two chains.

2. Piece in the usual manner.

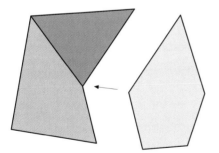

Method 2

1. Slit the paper up one of the seams to the "point" of the Y.

2. Place the first piece of fabric, right side up, on the shiny side of the freezer paper. Clip the seam allowance at the junction of the Y as shown. Be careful; do not clip too far.

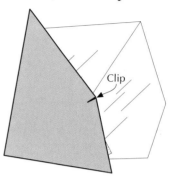

Clip

3. Place the adjoining piece, right sides together, on top of the first piece. Stitch, flip, and press. As each piece of fabric is added, clip its seam allowance right at the junction of the Y.

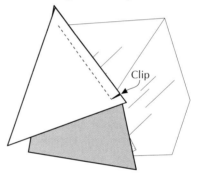

Clip

4. Place the third piece on top of the second piece, right sides together. Stitch, clip the seam allowance, flip, and press.

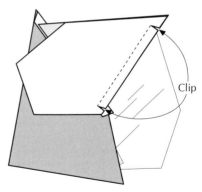

Clip

5. Carefully fold the pattern piece to line up the two edges of the slit, with the seam allowances right sides together. Pin the seam and sew from the center of the Y to the end of the slit.

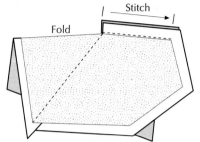

Fold   Stitch

Note: You can sew the pieces to the Y-seam section in any order you wish, but you must sew the seam along the slit last.

SEWING
THE
CHAINS
TOGETHER

Do not remove the foundation before sewing the chains together and do not staystitch around the chains after they are covered. Because each seam is a straight line, you won't need to ease curves.

The order of reassembly is much like that of simple piecing. Sew each straight section of a seam separately, beginning and ending the stitching line where it meets other seams.

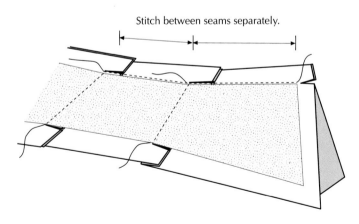

Stitch between seams separately.

1. Fold intersecting seam allowances back out of the way. Your work will lie flatter if you sew through no more than two layers of fabric at a time.

Note: Do not remove paper until *all* chains have been sewn together to make the complete top.

2. Pin, then stitch one section at a time. Pin each end of the section first. The ends should line up perfectly. If they do not, check to see that you are joining the correct sections together. Pin the middle of the section only if it is more than a few inches in length. Remember to keep the seam allowances of other seams free of the seam you are sewing.

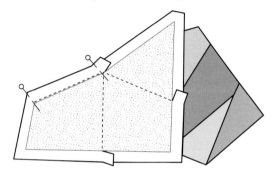

3. Sew the section between the pins. If a seam intersects the middle of a section, fold back the intersecting seam allowance where they cross. Stitch along the paper pattern; do not sew beyond into the seam allowances at the end of the section. This helps the work lie flatter.

4. When one section of seam is sewn, remove the pins and repeat steps 1–3 for the next section. Repeat for all chains.

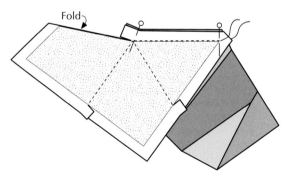

Fold

Note: Never try to pin and sew more than one straight section at a time. Pins placed in more than one section distort the pieces, making it harder to fit sections together.

PRESSING
THE
SEAMS

Press both seam allowances in the same direction; do not press them open. I often let the seam allowances lie naturally and press them that way, even if it means that not all of the seam allowances are pressed in the same direction.

To reduce bulk, press multiple seam allowances that meet at a point in a pinwheel around the point.

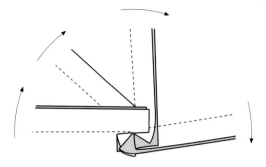

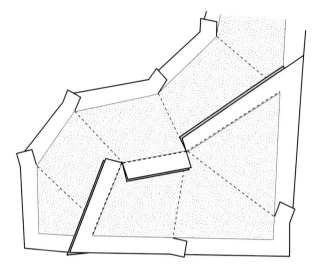

PROJECT:
OTTO

16½" x 16½"

Diane Ross created this charming creature as a gift for her friend, Julie Ketter, who has a dachshund named Otto. If you do not have the dachshund fabric on hand, substitute with other highly contrasting, neutral prints. Much of this quilt's snap is due to its high contrast.

Otto by Diane Ross, 1993, Woodinville, Washington, 16½" x 16½". Dachshund fabric adds detail to this charming family friend, Otto Frog. Collection of Julie Ketter.

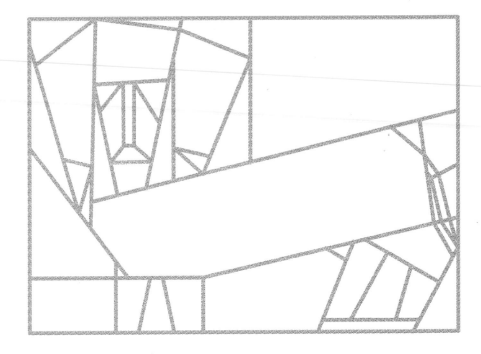

¼ yd. or scraps for background and checkerboard border

¼ yd. or scraps of dark brown for Otto's body and checkerboard border

Assorted scraps of light and medium brown fabrics for Otto's nose, ears, and legs

⅛ yd. of green dachshund fabric for upper and left side border

1 strip, 1½" x 13", dark green for lower border

18" x 18" square of backing

18" x 18" square of batting

¼ yd. for binding

10" x 13" rectangle of freezer paper for pattern

MAKING THE PATTERN

1. The pre-gridded image for "Otto" appears on page 111. Referring to "Using a Grid" on pages 95–96, make a cartoon measuring 8" x 11¼".

2. Lay the freezer paper over the cartoon, shiny side up. The heavy lines outline the chains of polygons. The light lines are the sew-and-flip lines. Trace the seam lines and sew-and-flip lines, being particularly careful to trace the tail accurately; small errors can really show here. Remember to extend the seam lines to the edge of the pattern.

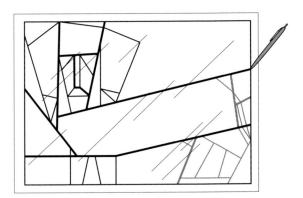

3. Turn the pattern over. On the matte side, mark the seam lines (both heavy and light), chain letters, and polygon numbers. In each chain, the polygons are numbered in the order that they are sewn onto the chain.

4. Trace the light seam lines onto the matte side of the freezer paper.

5. Cut the pattern apart on the heavy seam lines. Do not cut the light lines. Pin the pattern pieces to a sheet of paper to stay organized.

CUTTING AND APPLYING THE FABRIC

1. Following the directions given for polygonal chain piecing on pages 48–53, cover the polygons in each chain in the numerical order indicated. Clip the seam allowances and press.

2. Pin or set the pieces together as you finish covering them, to see how the design is developing.

ASSEMBLING THE QUILT TOP

1. Follow the suggested order or use your own sequence for sewing the chains together to make the quilt. Remember, when two chains are joined, pin first, then sew one straight section of the seam before moving on to the next section of the chain. Press seam allowances to one side.

2. Sew chain C to chain D. Add chain B, then chain E.

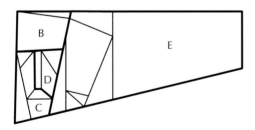

3. Sew chain H to chain I, being careful to align the seams forming the tail. Add chain G.

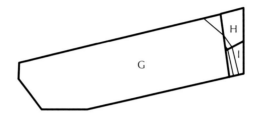

4. Sew the sections made in step 2 and 3 together. Sew chain A to the right side, then add chain F.

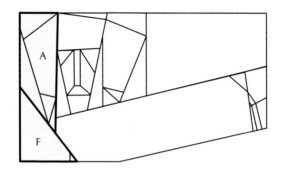

5. Sew chain J to chain K, then sew this section to the section made in step 4.

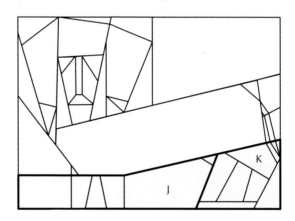

6. Press the entire panel.

7. Trim the panel to measure 11¾" x 8½".

8. From the background fabric, cut a 2¾" x 11¾" strip; sew this strip to the top of the panel. From the background fabric, cut a 2" x 11¾" strip; sew this strip to the bottom of the panel. Press the seam allowances open.

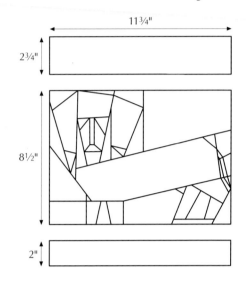

9. Cut a 1¾" x 12¼" strip from the dachshund border fabric. Sew to the left side of the quilt. Press seam allowances open.

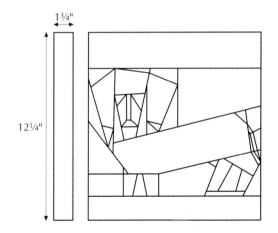

10. Sew the 1½" x 13" dark green lower border strip to the bottom of the quilt. From the dachshund border fabric, cut a strip, 3¾" x 13", then sew it to the top of the quilt. Press all seam allowances open.

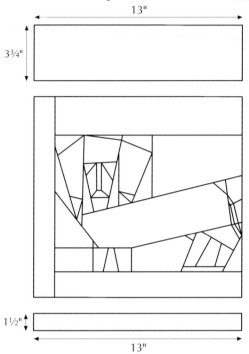

11. To make the checkerboard border, cut 3 background and 3 dark brown strips, each 1½" x 24". Sew the strips together as shown to make strip-pieced units. Press seam allowances toward the dark brown strips. Cut across the strips at 1½" intervals to make strip-pieced segments as shown.

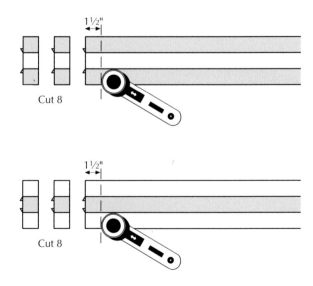

Cut 8

Cut 8

12. Sew the strip-pieced segments together, alternating units cut from each strip-pieced unit as shown. Press.

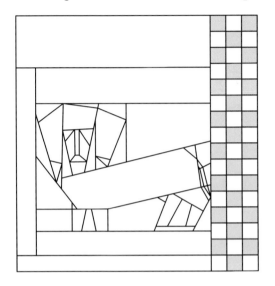

13. Sew the checkerboard border to the right side of the quilt. Press seam allowances open.

COMPLETING THE QUILT

Refer to Section 7, "From Top to Finish," on pages 101–9.

1. Mark the quilt as desired for quilting.

2. Layer the backing, batting, and quilt top. Baste.

3. Quilt by hand or machine. Diane machine quilted in-the-ditch (just beside the seam line).

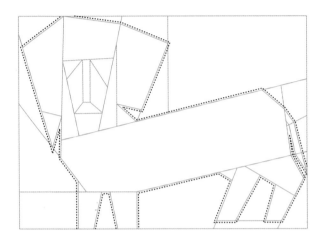

4. Square the quilt.

5. Bind the edges. (For double-fold binding, cut 2 strips, each 2" wide, across the width of the fabric from selvage to selvage.)

6. Label the quilt; sew on a hanging sleeve if desired. Share and enjoy!

Arcturus Moons by Mia Rozmyn, 1992,
Seattle, Washington, 36" x 43". Luminous
flowers by a pool appear to trail over
rising orange moons.

The one really important design feature to avoid is a polygon with a notch in its side.

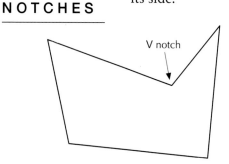

V notch

DESIGNING
WITH
POLYGONS

Quilters' rulers commonly come with 45°, 60°, and 90° angles marked on them, but making shapes only with these angles can be limiting. This chapter takes a fresh look at designing with polygons. The variety of traditional designs based on squares, rectangles, and triangles indicates how versatile polygons can be. Straight-line segments laid out properly can give the illusion of a curve or circle. Many small polygons, carefully shaded, can work together as a single visual element. When you lay out polygons on a cartoon and trace a pattern, little or no math is involved. Even for carefully controlled designs, such as Mariner's Compass or Pickle Dish, simple drafting techniques are substituted for complicated measurements.

To learn each of these techniques, try laying out some polygons on scratch paper, following the directions for each method. Once you have laid out the polygons and have made some notation about color and fabric choice, you will piece all of them in the same manner. (See "Polygonal Piecing" on pages 48–53.)

Sewing this shape is difficult because there is not enough fabric for a $1/4$"-wide seam allowance inside the inner corner of the notch. V notches can be easily avoided if all of the angles inside the polygon are less than 180° (a straight line is 180°). If you design a polygon with a V notch, either change its shape or split it into two polygons by adding a line through it.

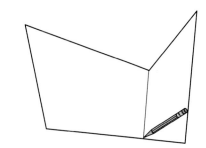

In network design, the polygons are created by first drawing points across the pattern, then drawing lines from point to point to determine the polygons' shapes. My personal term for this method is "connect the dots."

1. Take a piece of scratch paper and put a dozen or so dots on it. Spread them out randomly across the paper.

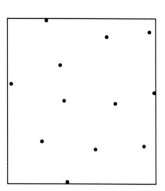

2. Connect the dots with straight lines, using a straight edge. While drawing the lines, keep an eye out for and eliminate V notches.

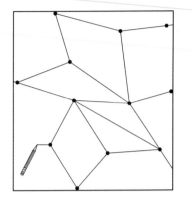

3. Connect some or all of the dots to form polygons. There is an almost infinite number of ways that you might connect them. Allow lines to cross (which will result in more polygons) or do not cross them; use many lines or just the minimum. Connect them to form triangles only, or create a combination of many-sided polygons. Notice that the angles and sides of the polygons are all different but always fit together. If you do this exercise several times, it's unlikely that any of your designs will be the same. Network design produces the most disorderly, random designs. It may remind you of a Crazy quilt.

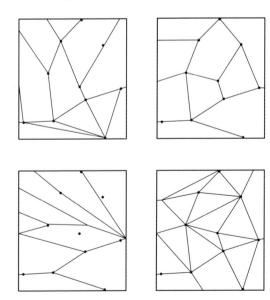

Other Design Possibilities

4. On another piece of scratch paper, lay out another dozen dots, but order them in some way. Try placing them in two lines or a rough circle. Connect the dots. If you connect them in a regular, systematic way, the resulting design will probably be less chaotic than the disorganized pattern you drew in step 3.

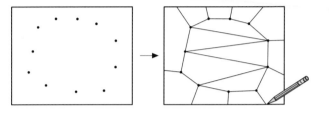

The way you lay out your dots and connect them has a strong influence on the visual texture of the design. Of course, color and fabric choices will further affect your design.

APPROXIMATING A CURVE

The next method is based on approximating curves by using multiple straight-line segments. On a piece of scratch paper, draw a circle 3" to 4" in diameter. It doesn't have to be a perfect circle, but if you want to trace around something round (your coffee mug?), it's okay.

The minimum number of sides that a polygon can have is three. Place three dots on the rim of the circle and connect them. Notice that the only parts of the line segments that actually touch the circle are the points where the lines meet. The remainder of the lines are inside the circle.

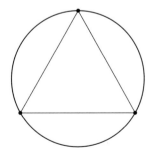

A triangle isn't a very good approximation of a circle. Draw another circle. This time, draw six or eight dots, equally spaced, around the edge of the circle. Connect the dots as shown.

As you can see from the illustration above, eight equally spaced sides start to look circular. Eight is a common number used in traditional optical illusion quilts, such as the Kaleidoscope pattern.

Now try another circle, but space your dots randomly along the line. When connected, they form a lumpy, uneven-looking circle. By manipulating the quantity and spacing of dots, you can achieve different effects.

On another piece of paper, trace the curve below.

Place eight or ten dots along the length of the curve and connect them.

In the illustration below left, notice that where I placed the dots closer together on the tighter parts of the curve, the lines connecting the dots approximate the curve better. These lines are shorter. The shallower the curve is, the longer the lines can be. With polygonal design, very tight curves can be difficult to approximate because the short seams become difficult to piece.

Up until now, only the ends of the lines have touched the curve. On any of the circle or line drawings you made in the steps at left, draw lines parallel to the original lines, but center them over the curve. The ends of the new lines will meet at points off the curve. This should make a better approximation of the curve.

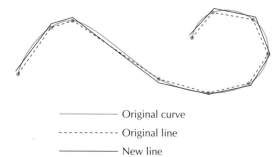

——————— Original curve

- - - - - - - - - - Original line

——————— New line

CONTROLLING THE ERROR

Drawing a line to represent a curve creates an area along the curve that is not perfectly included by the line. I call this area, the greatest distance between the straight-line segment and the curve, the "error." Here is a simple technique for controlling the maximum amount of error on a curve and quickly drawing a line to approximate that curve.

1. Draw a larger curve. This time, put one dot at one end of the curve.

2. For this example, limit the error to $\frac{1}{8}$", which means that the straight line you draw to connect two points on the curve won't lie more than $\frac{1}{8}$" from the line of the curve. For a straight edge, use a clear plastic ruler that has a $\frac{1}{4}$" line parallel to the edge, and $\frac{1}{8}$" marks between the $\frac{1}{4}$" line and the edge.

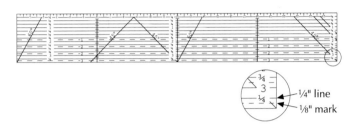

3. Lay the ruler over the curve, with one edge on the dot, and rotate it until the $\frac{1}{4}$" line just touches the curve. Make a dot where the edge of the ruler crosses the curve again.

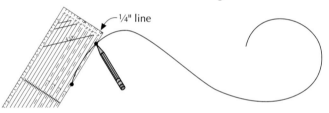

4. Place the $\frac{1}{8}$" marks on the ruler over these dots and draw a line along the ruler's edge. Be sure to draw the line long enough to intersect with the next line you draw.

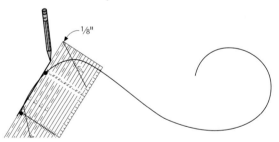

5. Place the edge of the ruler on the second dot, rotate it the way you did in step 3, and place the third dot where the ruler touches the line. Repeat the process until you have drawn lines to approximate the whole curve.

CREATING POLYGONS FROM CURVES

A curve represented with straight lines needs to be "fleshed out" to create polygons. You can do this by echoing the curve (repeating the same curve to make parallel curves), creating more than one curve and connecting them, or creating a grid of curves and connecting them. Another way to create polygons along a curve is to first create a connected arrangement of polygons, then draw a curve around the border and connect the curve's lines to the network of polygons.

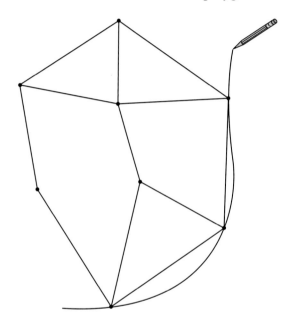

Connecting Curves to a Network

In the example block on page 48, I first drew a series of lines to approximate the curves of the original basic block on page 16 and then filled in the interior of the pieces with a network of polygons. This preserved the curves as distinct lines in the design. Only the insides of the areas were irregularly or randomly structured, much like a Crazy quilt.

Laying out polygons along curves aligns them and produces a more organized design. If I had drawn additional curves echoing the lines of the original curve, drawn dots along these echoing curves, and connected the dots, the block might have looked like this:

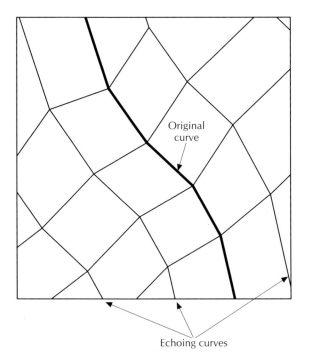

Original curve

Echoing curves

Connecting Echoing Curves

The moons in "Arcturus Moons" on page 60 are made of concentric circles that I divided into polygons as shown below. The rings or bands in the illustration are shaded to emphasize the concentric circles. For the moons in the quilt, fabric color and value placement within the polygons create the illusion of transparency.

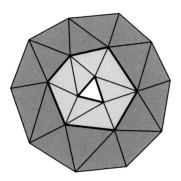

Connecting Grids of Curves

Another way to generate polygons from curves is by drawing curves that cross each other, marking a dot where they intersect, then drawing straight lines to connect the dots in order to approximate the curves. This is an excellent method for laying out quilts that have irregularly shaped blocks adapted from traditional right-angle (square or rectangular) blocks.

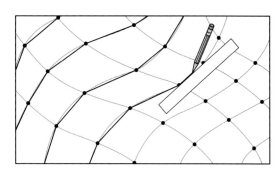

A Flowing Grid

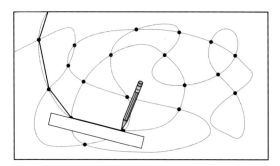

An Abstract Curve

CONVERTING IMAGES TO POLYGONS

If you want to lay out polygons that resemble something, such as a rose, a bird, or a mountain, sketch it first. The sketch doesn't have to be a da Vinci to work—just draw the general shape and the proportions of the image you want to create. Remember, you can adjust the lines as you work on the design.

Now place dots on the contours of the sketch. The contours are the lines of the sketch that outline the object's shape. Place dots at all places where lines cross. Place more dots in the interior of the sketch if needed to give the object form.

Connecting the Dots

Try to connect them as if each polygon represents a plane touching the surface of the image. For the flowers in "Arcturus Moons," I found that the petals had a more three-dimensional feel if I used more than one triangle for each petal. By making the triangles long and thin, extending from flower center to petal tip, the petals had a more graceful linear quality.

USING COLOR IN POLYGONAL DESIGN

The color and value layout affects the line and visual appearance of the design and can affect how you draw the polygons. If two polygons of a similar color are touching or share an entire side, they will read as part of the same shape. I call this joined color or bands of color. If they contrast with the polygons around them, they form a distinct line in the composition. Many string-pieced quilt patterns, such as Double Wedding Ring or Grandmother's Flower Garden, work this way.

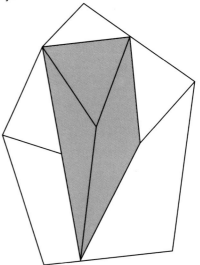

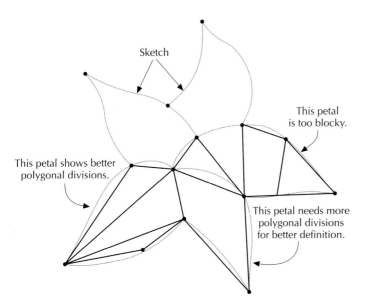

Sketch

This petal is too blocky.

This petal shows better polygonal divisions.

This petal needs more polygonal divisions for better definition.

If two similar polygons touch only at a corner, they form a chain of color. If they contrast with the polygons around them, they form a line in the composition, but the line will look "fuzzy," having jagged edges, not continuous ones. Trip Around the World, Ocean Waves, and Bargello patterns work this way. When many low-contrasting chains of color parallel each other, their edges tend to blur together.

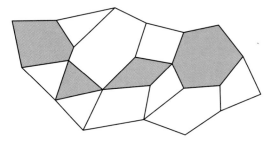

Obviously, if you want to design a particular line into your quilt, you need to decide whether you want it to be distinct or blurred. The illustration below shows the curves approximated as bands of color, with the polygons' edges laid out along the curves. Color or value groups of polygons joined in this manner work better for creating distinct edges.

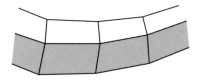

Chains of color or value blend or gradate the edges of an area. Most star patterns are chains of color. The illustration below shows similar outer curves and dots as the illustration below left, but the center curve and dots are eliminated. Polygons centered along the curves, their dots touching only the two outside curves instead, make the effect quite different from the joined-color curve.

In conclusion, this section is not intended to be a comprehensive survey of all of the possibilities but does attempt to present a few approaches for laying out polygons. Use one of these techniques or combine all of them in different parts of the same design. In "Arcturus Moons" on page 60, for example, I used "representational polygons" to lay out the branch and flowers. I broke up the sky area with "network polygons" to allow more texture and shading. "Band design polygons," used on the moons, give the moons subtle concentric rings and emphasizes their shape. The reeds are loosely based on polygonal chains of color.

PROJECT:
OBELISQUE

28" x 21"

I once read a book about composition written for watercolor painters in which the author described the way people "read" different forms. He said that long horizontal forms are associated with the horizon, landscape, and static elements and that vertical forms are associated with people and living things. I decided to use polygons to reduce horizontal and vertical forms to their simplest elements and see where the design would go. This quilt is the result.

As with any figure study, playing with color and value produces some interesting effects. I tied my figures together with a band of darker background. They seem less isolated that way, more communal. Interesting variations would be to place a diagonal shaft of light in the background to illuminate the figures or to isolate them from each other.

Simple changes in color or contrasts in value completely change the message of the quilt. The mood would have been much different had I created light figures against a dark ground or made some of the figures light and some dark.

MATERIALS   44"-WIDE FABRIC

³/₄ yd. total light fabric or scraps for center panel

Assorted medium to dark scraps for figures

¹/₂ yd. for border

²/₃ yd. for backing

24" x 29" rectangle of batting

¹/₄ yd. for binding

18" x 54" rectangle of freezer paper for pattern

Obelisque by Mia Rozmyn, 1994, Seattle, Washington, 28" x 21". Abstract figures people an empty landscape in this color and composition study.

MAKING THE PATTERN

1. Cut 2 pieces of freezer paper, each 18" x 22". Tape the long edges together, then trim to 22" x 27". Center the freezer paper, shiny side up, over the cartoon on the pullout pattern insert. Tape in place.

2. Prepare the freezer-paper pattern. (See "Making the Pattern" on page 16.) The heavy lines are the edges of the chains of polygons. Turn the freezer paper over to the matte side and mark the sew-and-flip lines and any notations you need to make.

3. Mark pattern letters on the chains and numbers indicating the piecing order along the chain if desired. Make any notations indicating color choices for the polygons. You do not need to draw registration marks.

4. Cut the pattern apart on the heavy lines.

5. Pin the pattern pieces to the cartoon to keep them organized.

CUTTING AND APPLYING THE FABRIC

1. Following the directions given for chain polygonal piecing on pages 48–53, cover the polygons in each chain in the numerical order indicated. Clip the seam allowances that you will sew over later when you join the chains. (See "Separating the Pattern into Chains" on pages 49–51.) You do not need to staystitch around the chains.

Note: Chain B has a Y seam. Refer to pages 51–52 for instructions on piecing Y seams.

2. Repin the chains to the cartoon as you finish covering them to see how the design is developing.

ASSEMBLING THE QUILT TOP

1. Follow the suggested order or use your own sequence for sewing the chains together to make the quilt. Remember, when two chains join together, pin first, then sew one straight section of the seam before moving on to the next section of the chain. Press seam allowances to one side.

2. Sew chain A to chain B. Sew chain J to chain P, then add chain K.

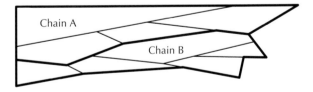

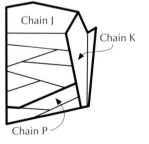

3. Sew chain D to J/K/P, then add chain L. Sew chain N to chain M, then add chain E.

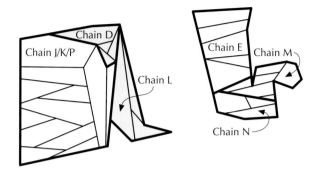

4. Sew chain G to chain M, then inset chain F. Sew chain H to chain I, then add to chain G.

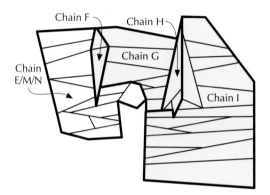

5. Inset chain O into M/N/G/I, then add A/B and inset chain C.

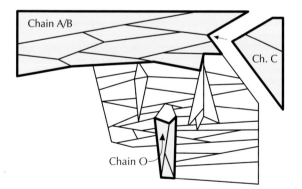

6. Sew chain D/L/J/K/P in place as shown. Sew chain Q to chain R, then attach Q/R to complete the quilt top.

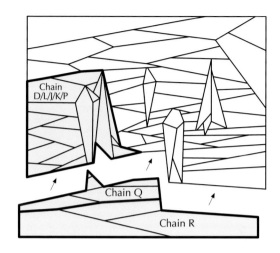

7. Press and square the completed top. (See "Squaring the Quilt" on pages 102–3.)

8. From border fabric, cut 4 strips, each 2" x 42". Measure across the quilt top from side to side. Cut 2 strips to this measurement and sew a strip to the top and bottom of the quilt top. Press the seam allowances open.

9. Measure the length of the quilt top, including the borders just added. Cut the 2 remaining strips to this length and sew a strip to each side of the quilt. Press the seam allowances open.

COMPLETING THE QUILT

Refer to Section 7, "From Top to Finish," on pages 101–9.

1. Mark the quilt as desired for quilting.

2. Layer the backing, batting, and quilt top. Baste.

3. Quilt by hand or machine. I quilted "Obelisque" with curving horizontal lines that represent wind.

4. Square the quilt.

5. Bind the edges.

6. Label the quilt; sew on a hanging sleeve if desired. Share and enjoy!

Mama's Crane by Mia Rozmyn, 1991, Seattle, Washington, 28" x 28". In this piece about paralysis and hope, a lone crane escapes into the dawn from an empty, beautiful marble terrace.

COMBINING TECHNIQUES

This section discusses combining all of the foundation techniques covered in the first sections of the book, then adding rotary-cut, strip-pieced fabrics and appliqué.

Each of the techniques described in the first sections can be used alone to make lovely quilts as can any combination of them. The real strength of foundation piecing from a cartoon and pattern lies in its flexibility.

COMBINING FOUNDATION TECHNIQUES

As you draw the cartoon for a design, plan how you will combine foundation-piecing techniques. Plan each technique where it best suits the needs of the design. Remember to put registration marks on curved seams and staystitch the pieces before you remove the paper.

My "United Colors of Penguin" quilt on page 80 combines three foundation techniques with appliqué: simple piecing and appliqué for the penguins, polygonal piecing for the sky, and string piecing for some of the polygons.

In general, you will find it necessary to complete string piecing and polygonal piecing *before* sewing the curved pieces (simple piecing).

DOUBLE

PATTERNING

Some designs are easier to piece if you make two patterns. I call this double patterning. Use this to eliminate errors that may accumulate before they become large problems. For example, in a pattern that is divided into sections, if each section is sewn too small (or too large), the total error, multiplied by the number of sections, would be significant enough to cause problems when placing the sections into the rest of the design.

To use the double-patterning technique, cut the first pattern as usual. Piece the small areas of the pattern to make larger units. Cut the second pattern into these larger units and compare them to the pieced units. Then, correct any errors accumulated in the first pattern pieces before assembling them using the second pattern.

Consider the design below. The circle is divided into eight wedges to be individually string-pieced with triangles.

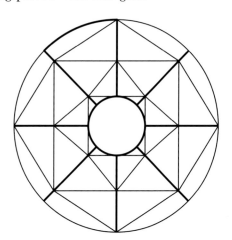

1. Cut the first pattern into wedges, then string-piece them.

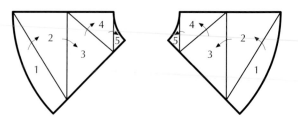

Note: If each of the eight seams joining the wedges are as little as $1/16$" off, the total error around the circle adds up to 1". Making a second pattern identifies and eliminates this error factor.

2. Slit the second pattern on one seam line only, then string-piece the second pattern, using the completed wedges as "strings."

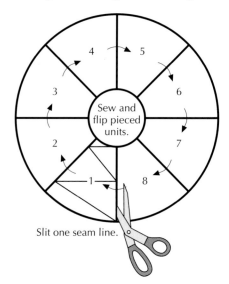

This method works very well with Mariner's Compass designs.

You can use double patterning for bed-size quilts, but be aware of potential problems. The tendency in foundation piecing is to sew slightly off the edge of the foundation, so that even minor errors can accumulate. In unique designs with seams going in many directions, this causes distortion, especially if the quilt is large. The quilt top may not lie flat or seams may not line up.

You can compare the parts of the quilt to the original cartoon to catch errors instead of making a second pattern, although sometimes this is awkward if the piece is very large.

COMBINING FOUNDATION PIECING WITH STRIP PIECING

You can iron any foundation pattern piece onto a "fabric" made of several fabrics strip-pieced together, then cut and use it as one piece in a quilt. Doing this saves considerable time. "Untitled" on page 101 by Kathleen O'Hanlon and "Tea Garden" on page 42 combine these methods.

You don't need to draw every strip-pieced seam onto your cartoon, just make enough notations so that you can align the pattern piece properly. This is particularly true if you must cut many pattern pieces from strip-pieced fabric and use the seams for lining up the pieces.

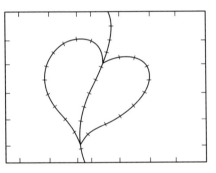

Registration marks show where to align seams.

USING FOUNDATION INSETS

Sometimes, you can sew a small area of foundation piecing into a unit more quickly by using another technique. In this case, sew an area of foundation piecing into a larger piece using an inset. This method comes in handy when repairing damaged areas on a quilt or when changing or improving small areas that are already pieced.

For practice, machine piece a heart into an already-pieced quilt top without appliquéing it.
1. Draw a cartoon of the heart, using the heart template above right.

2. Trace a pattern of the heart on the freezer paper's shiny side. Draw a 5" x 5" square around it for background. Add registration marks on the matte side as shown.

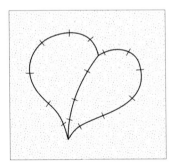

3. Carefully cut apart the pattern. If you cut the background pattern to get to the heart, tape it back together.

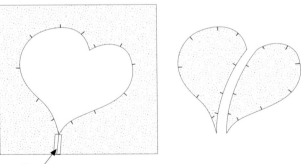

Tape

4. With the shiny side of the freezer paper against the wrong side of the background fabric, place the background pattern piece where you want the heart to be.

Wrong side of background fabric

TIP If your background is pieced, place the point and notch of the heart on a seam to avoid a V notch.

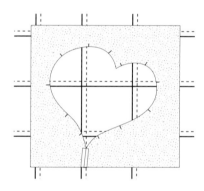

5. Iron the background pattern in place. Iron the heart pattern pieces to the wrong side of the heart fabrics. On the background fabric, staystitch in the "hole" where the heart pieces will go. Do not staystitch along the line dividing the heart pieces. Staystitch around the heart halves. Clip registration marks.

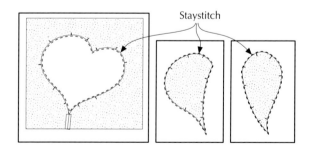

Staystitch

6. Trim away the background fabric inside the stay stitching, leaving enough fabric for a seam allowance. Clip registration marks on the background. Remove the background pattern.

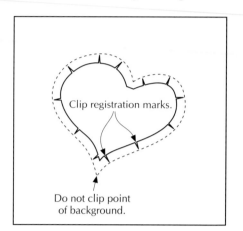

Clip registration marks.

Do not clip point of background.

7. Sew the two sides of the heart together.

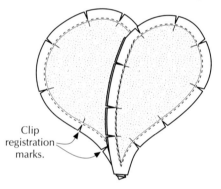

Clip registration marks.

8. Working from the wrong side of the sample and on only one heart half at a time, match registration marks, pin, and sew the heart to the background, right sides together. (See "Simple Piecing" on pages 16–23.) Appliqué tip of heart.

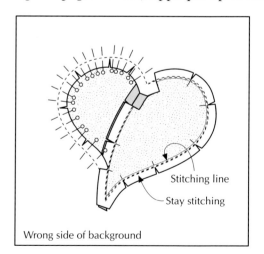

Stitching line

Stay stitching

Wrong side of background

COMBINING FOUNDATION PIECING WITH APPLIQUÉ

Many charming designs that combine strip-pieced backgrounds with appliqué appear in current publications. A large appliqué design can be machine pieced using the foundation inset technique. If the foundation design is a small area of the quilt, insetting saves a lot of paper.

The same design limitations apply in insetting as in simple piecing. Make curves larger than 1" in diameter and avoid V notches. Some designs may require combining foundation machine piecing with foundation appliqué. Small curves and sharp points lend themselves easily to appliqué. Save considerable time by machine piecing part of the design; then, leaving the freezer paper on the pieces, appliqué the areas that you can't machine piece. This allows more design flexibility.

Most of the design for "Iris Moon" on page 28 requires simple piecing. However, some of the curves on the petals can be difficult. The more difficult a seam is to piece, the longer it takes, removing the advantage to machine piecing. Appliqué becomes a "shortcut" in this case.

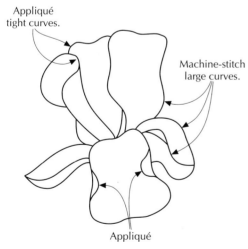

Appliqué tight curves.

Machine-stitch large curves.

Appliqué

If you want to use appliqué in "Iris Moon," you do not need to change the cartoon and pattern. Cut out the pieces and staystitch as usual, then hand sew some of the sections instead of machine piecing them.

Look at "United Colors of Penguin" on page 80. The color spots on the penguins' faces are too small to machine piece, so I recommend appliquéing them.

1. Place the freezer paper with the shiny side up, on the pattern for the penguin's face. Trace the penguin's face and color spots on the shiny side of the freezer paper. Retrace the color spots on the matte side.

2. Cut out the freezer-paper pattern. Do not cut out the color spots. Iron the pattern piece onto the *wrong* side of the penguin's face fabric, cut out the fabric, leaving a ¼"-wide seam allowance, and staystitch around it. (See "Stay Stitching" on pages 19–20.) Clip registration marks.

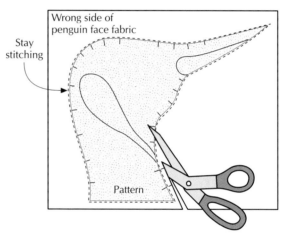

Wrong side of penguin face fabric

Stay stitching

Pattern

3. Peel away the paper from the fabric, then from this pattern, cut out the two color-spot patterns. Iron the color spot patterns onto the wrong side of the correct fabric, then cut out the pieces, leaving a ¼"-wide seam allowance all around. Staystitch color spot and clip, then remove paper pattern.

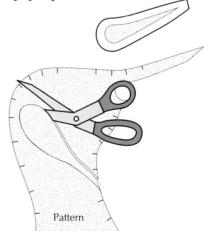

Pattern

4. Lay the used face pattern, shiny side up, onto the penguin's face and move each color spot into position under the face pattern, then pin in place. Remove the face pattern, but leave the color spots pinned in place.

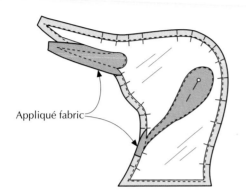

Appliqué fabric

5. Turn under each color spot's seam allowance, including the stay stitching. Blindstitch in place or appliqué, using your favorite method.

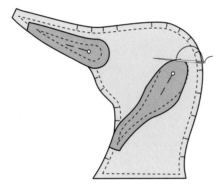

USING DOUBLE PATTERNING FOR APPLIQUÉ

The appliquéd hearts in the illustration below overlap machine-pieced seams. The dashed line shows the seam that lies behind the appliqué.

Double patterning (page 74) works well for a design such as this. Draw one pattern showing only the machine-pieced seams with notations to position the appliqué hearts.

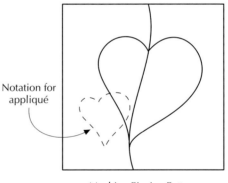

Notation for appliqué

Machine Piecing Pattern

Draw a second pattern for the appliqué pieces.

Appliqué Pattern

USING
APPLIQUÉ

Use appliqué to avoid V notches. Look at the leaf in the illustration below. Everything machine pieces gracefully except for the tip of the leaf.

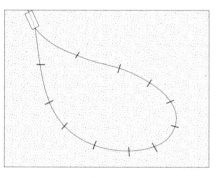

Cartoon

1. Cut out the leaf as an inset. (See "Using Foundation Insets" on pages 75–76.)

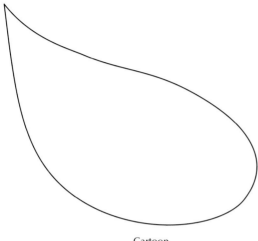

Pattern

2. Staystitch the leaf and background as outlined in the steps on page 76. Trim away the background fabric, keeping the $1/4$"-wide seam allowance. Do not clip the seam allowance in the background at the tip of the leaf. Sew as much of the leaf as you can sew easily on the machine.

Start and stop machine stitching here.

Stay
stitching

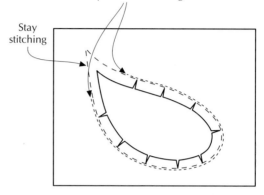

3. Turn the piece over and turn under the remaining seam allowances, then appliqué tip.

Turn under seam allowance.

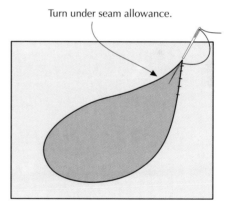

United Colors of Penguin by Mia Rozmyn, 1994,
Seattle, Washington, 37" x 24". In this playful version
of the gray Antarctic, colorful penguins parade across
a fertile landscape before a vivid sky.

PROJECT: UNITED COLORS OF PENGUIN

37" x 24"

One Christmas, the National Geographic Society sent out a photo postcard showing parading penguins. I was so intrigued by them that I was inspired to make this quilt. When I chose fabric for the penguins, I found that black and white and orange just didn't appeal to me. Colored penguins are more fanciful. The stripes in the sky fabrics give the pieced pinwheel swirls much more character. All of the fabrics are cotton.

MATERIALS   44"-WIDE FABRIC

1 yd. or scraps of orange, pink, and green stripes for sky

½ yd. or scraps of blue-green for ground

¼ yd. each of green, red, and burgundy for penguin backs and heads

⅛ yd. each of pale orange, mauve, and pink for penguin fronts

⅛ yd. or scraps of orange, teal, and green for penguin color spots

⅛ yd. or scraps of gray for inner border

½ yd. orange stripe for outer border

⅞ yd. for backing

28" x 40" rectangle of batting

¼ yd. or scraps for binding

18" x 32" rectangle of freezer paper for pattern

MAKING THE PATTERN

1. Center the freezer paper, shiny side up, over the cartoon on the pullout pattern insert. Tape in place.

2. Prepare the freezer-paper pattern. (See "Making the Pattern" on page 17.) The heavy lines outline the edges of the pattern pieces. The light lines are the sew-and-flip lines.

3. Mark the pattern letters on the chains, mark the numbers indicating the polygons' piecing order along the chain, and draw registration marks where they meet curved seams. Make any notations indicating color choices for the polygons. Mark pattern numbers and registration marks on simple pieced areas.

4. Cut the pattern apart on the heavy seam lines. Do not cut the light lines. When you cut out the penguin faces, do not separate the color spots from the head piece. This will be done later.

5. Pin the pattern pieces to the cartoon to keep them organized.

CUTTING AND APPLYING THE FABRIC

1. Starting with the pinwheel swirls, cut strips of fabric wide enough to cover any of the strings in the swirl. Remember to add ¼"-wide seam allowances on both sides of the string. String-piece the strips to each swirl, following the numerical order given on the pullout pattern. (See "String Piecing" on pages 34–41.) Treat each swirl as a chain later when piecing them into the sky.

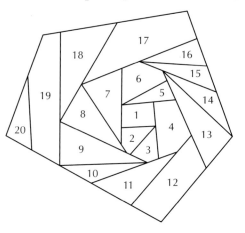

2. For each of the penguin and ground pieces, cut the pattern apart, then iron the pattern, shiny side down, onto the wrong side of the fabric. (See "Attaching the Pattern Pieces to the Fabric" on page 19.)

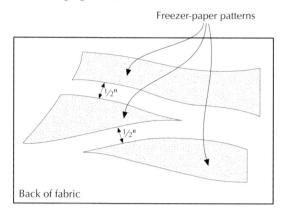

Freezer-paper patterns

1/2"

1/2"

Back of fabric

3. Cut out the fabric pieces, leaving 1/4"-wide seam allowances beyond the pattern edge.

4. Staystitch around each piece and clip the registration marks.

5. Pin the pattern pieces up on the wall so that you can see how they work together.

6. For the polygonal sky chains, follow the directions given for chain polygonal piecing on pages 48–53, covering the polygons in each sky chain in the numerical order indicated. Clip the seam allowances that you will sew over when you join the chains. (See "Separating the Pattern into Chains" on pages 49–51.)

Note: Chains B and F have Y joints. If these bother you, cut one of the polygons off of the pattern, and treat it as a separate chain. (See "Piecing a Y Seam" on pages 51–52.)

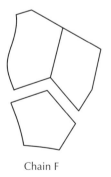

Chain F

7. Staystitch the curved edges of the chains where they attach to simple piecing and clip registration marks.

ASSEMBLING THE QUILT TOP

1. Following the instructions given in steps 1–3 on page 77 for "Combining Foundation Piecing with Appliqué," appliqué the color spots on the penguin faces.

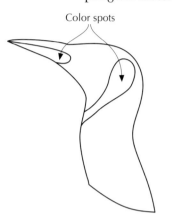

Color spots

2. Following the suggested order given or one of your own, begin sewing the pieces together. Remember to press each seam as it is sewn.

Note: Refer to the piecing order given with each diagram. For example, 1 + 2 + 3 means to sew piece 1 to piece 2 , then add piece 3. A section made of several pieces sewn together is enclosed by parentheses (1–3). Sometimes a section is sewn together, then one or more pieces are added to the section. For example, if pieces 1, 2, and 3 must be sewn into a section first, then pieces 9 and 22 added to this section, the instruction is (1–3) + 9 + 22. Two sections sewn together are indicated by (1–3) + (12–15).

3. Left penguin and ground:

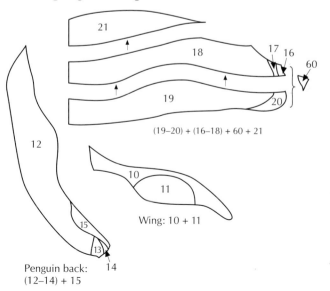

21

18

17 16

60

19

20

(19–20) + (16–18) + 60 + 21

12

10

11

Wing: 10 + 11

15

13

Penguin back: 14
(12–14) + 15

4. Center penguin:

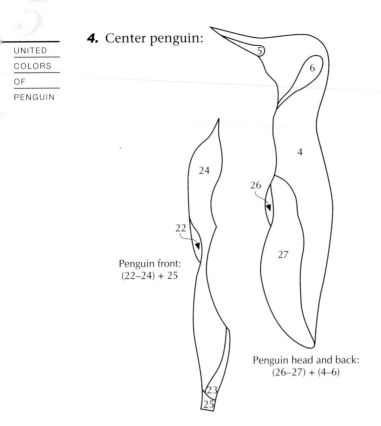

Penguin front:
(22–24) + 25

Penguin head and back:
(26–27) + (4–6)

5. Between the center and right penguins, assemble ground and foot sections.

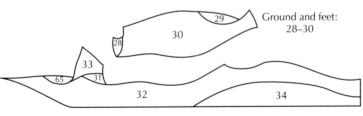

Ground and feet: (31 + 32 + 34) + 33 + 65

6. At the left side of the quilt and between the center and left penguins, assemble ground, left penguin, and sky sections.

7. In the center and on the right side of the quilt, assemble ground sections.

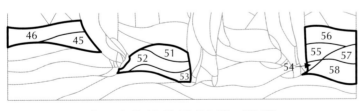

Ground: 45–46; 51–53; (54–56) + (57–58)

8. Assemble the sky chains and swirls on each side of the left penguin. Do not sew chain E to chain A or sew to penguin yet.

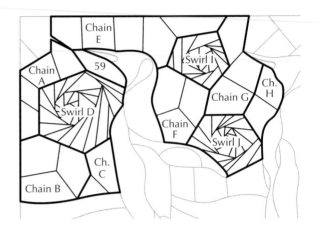

9. Sew chain M to swirl N, and chain O to swirl P.

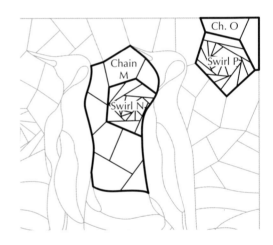

10. Sew together chains Q–T, then sew to swirl P. Sew 49 to (K, 48–47), then add 50.

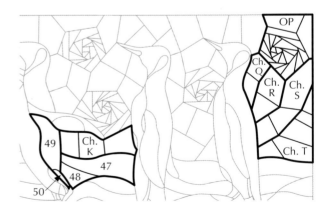

11. Assemble left sky, ground, and penguin front sections.

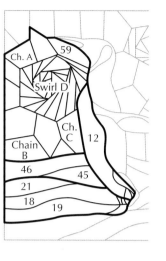

Sky, ground, and penguin:
(A–D, 59) + (45–46) +
(16–21) + (12–15)

12. Assemble left penguin back and wing, center sky, and ground.

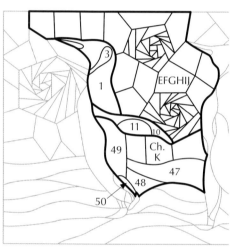

Penguin, sky, wing, and ground:
(1–3) + (E–J) + (10–11) + (K, 47–50)

13. Sew sky and upper ground sections between center and right penguins.

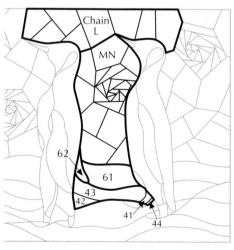

L + (M–N) + 61 + 62 + (41–44)

14. Assemble lower ground sections between center and right penguins and add to the section made in step 13.

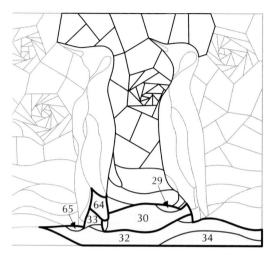

Sky and ground:
(31–34 + 63 + 65) + (28-30) +
(L–N, 41–44, 61–62) + 64

15. To the section made in step 14, add penguin front 37–39, leg 40, and ground pieces 36 and 66.

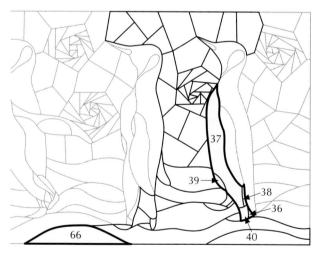

Penguin and ground: (37–39) + 40 + 36 + 66

16. Assemble right penguin back, then set into the section made in step 15.

Penguin back: (7–9) + 35

18. Assemble the center penguin, then set it into the right section of the quilt.

(22–24) + 25 + 26 + 27 + (4–6)

17. Sew right sky and ground sections to right penguin.

Sky and ground: (O–T) + (54–58) + right center section

19. Sew the section assembled in step 11 to the center section assembled in step 12. Add foot 67, then set in chain U.

20. Sew ground 68 to ground 69, then sew to section 51–53. Sew to the bottom of the section made in step 19.

21. Sew left quilt section to right quilt section.

ADDING THE BORDERS

1. Square the quilt top. (See "Squaring the Quilt" on pages 102–3.)

2. Cut 4 strips, each 1" wide, from inner border fabric. Measure through the center of the quilt from top to bottom and cut 2 strips to this length, then sew a strip to each side of the quilt.

3. Measure through the center of the quilt from side to side including the borders you just added. Cut the remaining 2 strips to this length, then sew a strip to the top and bottom of the quilt.

4. Following the directions for inner border strips in steps 2 and 3, measure, cut and sew 4"-wide outer border strips to the sides of the quilt, then to the top and bottom of the quilt.

5. Press the quilt top.

COMPLETING THE QUILT

Refer to Section 7, "From Top to Finish," on pages 101–9.

1. Mark the quilt as desired for quilting. I quilted swirling lines to represent wind in the sky, stippled the ground, and gave the penguins pin stripes.

2. Layer the backing, batting, and quilt top. Baste.

3. Quilt by hand or machine.

4. Square the quilt.

5. Bind the edges. I cut 4 strips, each 1½" wide, and used the single-fold binding technique.

6. Label the quilt. Sew on a hanging sleeve if desired. Share and enjoy!

The Artist *by Mia Rozmyn, 1994, Seattle, Washington, 31" x 49". My son Geoffrey at work.*

DEVELOPING YOUR OWN PATTERN

This section covers idea sources, design processes, and enlarging techniques.

There are few thrills in quilting like developing an original pattern from scratch and having it fall together beautifully into a quilt. This process begins with drafting your own pattern.

Drafting isn't really the best word for this process. It conjures up an image of precision and high-tech skills. This isn't exactly what happens. Pattern development, which is a repetitive process of trial, test, and adaptation, is probably a better term. The pattern may begin as a photo, a sketch, or a doodle.

DEVELOPING AN IDEA

All designs start from an idea. The idea is not necessarily complex and fully developed. It may be as simple as, "I like roses. I want to make a rose quilt," or "Mama, make me a rainbow quilt."

During the design process, the idea may grow and change or stay fairly stable. The important thing is to be open to the idea and let it change and improve if necessary. A design process that allows for modifications is invaluable.

Visibility is another important part of the design process. It is necessary to see the design so that you can interact with it. It is not un-usual for a minor part of the design to suddenly leap out at you once the design is drafted. When this happens, it may set off a whole chain of new ideas. If something is wrong with the design, you're much more likely to catch it if you have an accurate representation in front of you.

Where do ideas come from? I believe that art is an intrinsic part of being human. As humans, we sense the world around us and process these impressions in our brains. Our response to this synthesis is art.

We are not cameras, so our drawings may not look like the subject we're drawing. How well they match isn't the point. It is what we add as humans that makes an image art. To create images or designs or to "get an idea," we need to observe and think about the world around us. This may be the natural world or our cultural environment. It may be concrete, tangible things, or concepts and the symbols we associate with them.

If you want to make an original quilt, but your personal muse is out to lunch, here are some tricks to try. Start collecting images you like. Some people suggest starting a file, although I find that counterproductive. What good will an image do in a file? Hang images all over your house or office. Place them so that they are the first thing you see in the morning and the last thing at night. Put them where you'll see them at breakfast, instead of the cereal box or milk carton!

In our "Information Age," we have more access to art and graphics than any other generation. Immerse yourself in images, but don't let them grow stale or you'll quit seeing them. Move them around. Change them. Really look at them.

Check out library books on techniques for other art media. Read books on watercolor design, photography, architecture, and ceramics. How do other media approach design? What do they look for in composition, line form, and color? Learn some of the terms and concepts used in other disciplines, such as positive and negative space (foreground/background), landscape (horizontal) and vertical formats, and cropping (cutting away portions of the design).

Sit down with a handful of your favorite images and ask yourself what they have in common and how they differ.

My Favorite Images

How do the images address color, texture, and contrast? Are they in a vertical or landscape format? Do the designs fill the image, or is there lots of empty space? Where is the focal point or important information; is it a distant, middle, close, or "bury-your-nose-in-it" viewpoint? Are the images monochromatic (represented in values of one color)? Are they dark, rich colors or pastels? Are there multiple objects or single ones? Are they quiet and still or do they impart a feeling of motion?

Once you have made some observations about what you like, you have a guide to the type of design with which you'll be happiest. When I worked through this exercise, I discovered that I liked simple, closeup, single-object images in a vertical format with lots of deep, rich, highly contrasting colors, surrounded by empty space. I use this information to challenge myself to work in other formats and color groups. Sometimes we benefit the most by the greatest challenges. Stretch your wings!

For another exercise, make a mark on a piece of paper. Lay out a piece of cartoon paper the size of the finished quilt. Start with a small design, perhaps the size of a piece of typing paper. Small designs are easier to toss in the round file!

Tape the cartoon to the table. Place the pencil point on the paper. Close your eyes and make a mark. (Flat, white voids can be very intimidating!)

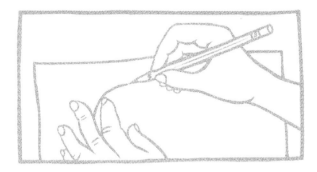

Once the surface has a mark on it, it's much easier to work on it. Even if you erase the mark, the page won't intimidate you any longer; the void has been broached. Just draw some curves. Let your imagination go. Play. It doesn't have to represent anything. As adults, we often expect too much of ourselves. We expect show quilts from class samples. We want our homework to read like Tolstoy or look like a da Vinci. Give yourself a chance to learn the piecing techniques, to get used to original work. I don't like some of my first pieces now, but other people still love them.

MAKING AN IDEA TANGIBLE

The process of pattern making is one of translation. We make quilts from discrete pieces of fabric with seams forming the boundaries. Some of these seam lines may contribute major composition lines to the image. Some may outline low-contrasting fabrics that provide the image's shading or texturing. Others may simply aid construction and are almost invisible.

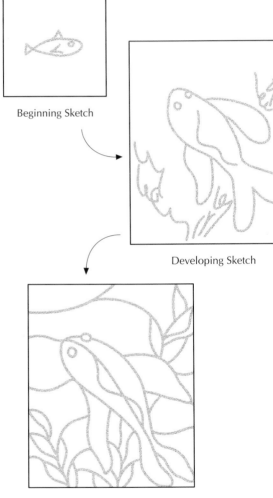

Beginning Sketch

Developing Sketch

Final Drawing with Seam Lines

Sketching

Once you have an idea, try to make it tangible by sketching it. Sketch it? Yes, I hear you. You think you can't draw either!

I've never had any formal art training. Lack of formal art training doesn't mean that we aren't artists. It means we're self-taught. Remember, it isn't how much the finished product looks like the original that counts; it's how we create it.

If you really can't make it look like what you see in your head, remember that you're working with paper and pencil. Maybe you need a crayon or maybe you only need practice—purchase a book about sketching and practice your drawing.

Set aside five to fifteen uninterrupted minutes each day to make a quick sketch. These are finger exercises. They don't even have to be legible or worked on expensive paper with fancy pencils. Quick sketches will train your eye and hand. Persevere! Give it time.

Don't expect the sketches to be more than they are. Draw anything—the mug on your desk, your shoes on the floor, faces from magazine articles—but draw! Draw something from your mind's eye or from memory. As you draw, you will start looking at and observing the world around you differently.

My eight-year-old son draws for hours every day. He never seems to get tired of it. Encounters with anything new send him back to his drawing. I think it's how he processes life. I've never seen him draw something that's in front of him. He only draws from his imagination.

Drawing by Geoffrey Rozmyn

Photographing

Many designers who don't want to sketch turn to photography. Photography makes an image tangible. If you want to make a pattern of a particular flower, take a slide of it. I recommend a slide over a snapshot because a projector can enlarge an image very effectively.

A photo can be the inspiration for a design. Remember, when you draft the actual pattern, you can alter the image to suit yourself.

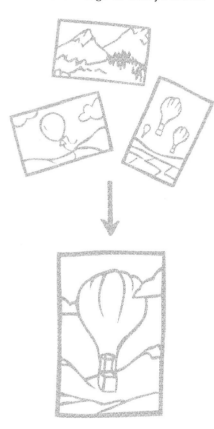

Sometimes photography is used to pirate other people's images. Unless a great deal of the image is changed, copying a design from a photograph may be a copyright infringement. I have seen quilts in shows that were direct copies of designs from paintings, children's books, and other sources. Even though they were remade in another medium, it was still plagiarism.

Be very careful about copying photographs. Check first to see if the image is copyrighted. If it is, write to the copyright holder for permission. This may be all that is necessary. If you have used an idea or an image for your design, please have the courtesy to give credit to the originator for the design or inspiration.

CALCULATING THE QUILT'S DIMENSIONS

Changing the size of the image to the quilt's finished size is probably the most tedious part of pattern making. Methods for changing the size of the image include freehand sketching and working with high-tech photocopy machines. Regardless of the method you use, there are a couple of preliminary steps.

First decide what size the quilt must be. Base your decision upon where you want to use the quilt, how much fabric you have, and how much time you want to spend on the work. Decide what the maximum reasonable dimensions can be. These height and width limitations may not represent the same proportions as your starting image. If they differ, you must decide whether to crop the image or alter the size to be able to keep the same proportions.

PHOTOGRAPH BY EDWARD J. ROZMYN

For instance, if I make a wall hanging based on the 8" x 10" photo above for my living room, I have one particular wall in mind on which to hang it. The space available is 64" high by 55" wide.

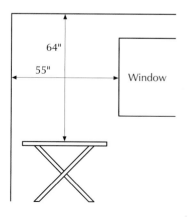

64"

55"

Window

To enlarge the dimensions of an image, multiply both the height and the width by the same number. This number is called the scale factor. If I were to enlarge the 8" x 10" image 5½ times, it would be 5½ times as wide and 5½ times as high, or 44" high by 55" wide. These dimensions would fill the width of the available wall space, but not the height.

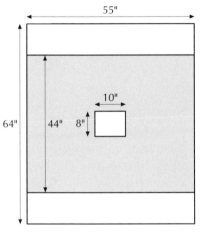

1":5½" scale

Since the boys are the actual focus of the photo and the rocks fill a large area of the background, I could choose to crop the image, making the image of the boys more important. If I wanted to fill the wall space, I could make the quilt 64" by 55" and only work with a $6\frac{5}{8}$"-wide portion of the photo, using a scale factor of 8".

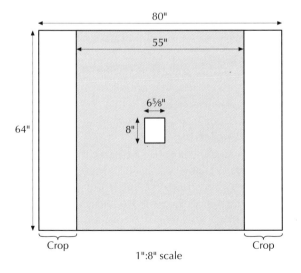

1":8" scale

To determine your own scale factor, divide the maximum possible width of the quilt by the width of the image (55" ÷ 10" = 5.5 or 5½).

This will give you one possible scale factor. Now divide the maximum possible height of the quilt by the height of the image (64" ÷ 8" = 8). This gives you a second scale factor. If the two scale factors are equal, you are ready to begin the enlarging process. If they are different, you must choose which factor you want to use (5½ or 8 for this example).

Using the smaller factor (5½) keeps the enlarged pattern in the same proportions as the original, but the quilt will not fill the maximum height and width. Using the larger factor (8) requires cropping the image to fit within the space available.

You can also choose a scale factor between these two extremes. You must crop the image if you use any factor with a number greater than the smallest factor (any number greater than 5½ for this example). Nice, round numbers make the easiest scale factors to use.

To keep the original proportions of the photo for the quilt in the example above, the scale factor must be 5½.

If you plan to use an opaque or slide projector to enlarge your image, first try cutting and taping the paper for the cartoon to make the maximum dimensions possible for the quilt. Later, when you project the image on the paper, you can adjust the image until you are satisfied with the results.

After you have decided on the size of the finished quilt, trim the cartoon to measure 2" longer and 2" wider than the finished quilt dimensions. The extra 2" allows you to extend the quilt's design beyond the image area so that you have enough fabric left to trim when squaring the quilt top. (See "Squaring the Quilt" on pages 102–3.) For the example quilt, after you add 2" to each dimension, the paper for the cartoon must measure 46" by 57".

If your quilt design is square or rectangular, make sure that each corner of your cartoon is a 90° angle. Mark these angles using a T square, a straight edge, or a good-quality quilting guide.

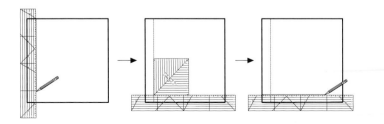

Choose a firm, smooth work surface at least as big as the paper. Tape the cartoon paper to the work surface. If you are using a projection method of enlargement, this will be a vertical surface. For the other methods, either a vertical or horizontal surface will do. For full-size quilts, I roll up my living room rug and work on the floor.

SKETCHING THE IMAGE

If you are working from a photo, enlarge it to at least 8" x 10", if possible, although you may find it easier to sketch a photo and enlarge the sketch. Try a photocopy enlargement; the result may lose some definition, but the proportions will be accurate.

Lay a piece of tracing paper, clear mylar, or drafting acetate over the photo. Using the same pen that you use to draw on freezer paper, trace any detail that seems even remotely important in the picture. Remember, you can delete lines later, but now is the easiest time to add them.

Draw the first lines to delineate any high-contrast breaks in the image. For the photo on page 92, outline the edges of the rocks and the boys.

Next, outline any areas that share the same or similar colors. Add more lines to shaded contour areas and gradual changes in value or color. Add lines to give the feel of texture.

This is a good time to make any changes in the image. When I designed "The Nesting Place of the Shen Lung" on page 13, I deleted much of the original image and added other elements. Because these tracings are easy to do, try making several and playing with different ideas. Keep yourself open to the image. Even a tracing that turns out to be a blind alley can give you more confidence in what you're doing. You'll then know one approach not to continue!

ENLARGING THE SKETCH

After you complete your sketch and are happy with the design, choose a method to enlarge it to fit the finished size. Some methods require special equipment, which may be expensive or have technical limitations. Others require no special equipment but are tedious.

Freehand Sketching

I prefer to simply draw the full-size design freehand on the cartoon. I like the look freehand drawing gives to a pattern. I think the time spent pondering a drawing and optimizing the lines is time well spent. From the process, I learn something about the image itself and what it says to me. I don't receive the same feedback when I use the other techniques that follow.

Photocopying

Save considerable time and effort with the clever use of a good photocopy machine. Some photocopy machines enlarge up to blueprint sizes. Check each photocopy carefully to make sure the image is not distorted.

Decide on the finished size of the design before you begin photocopying. Break down oversized designs into smaller sections and make several enlargements. Tape the final enlargements together to form a cartoon. Where the cartoon is taped together, check for and redraw any lines that don't meet.

The photocopy enlargement process does not work as well for photos as it does for line drawings and can be one of the more expensive methods of enlarging your design.

Using an Opaque Projector

Through the magic of lights and mirrors, an opaque projector projects an image onto a wall or screen. To use an opaque projector, you must have a wall for pinning or taping up your cartoon and a darkened room. On many machines, the enlargement ratio (scale factor) is limited, the focus is poor, and the size limit for the image is no larger than 8" x 10". To reduce distortion of the image, make sure your original lies flat on the machine and that the projector sits squarely on the floor without being tilted. Make sure that the image is projected straight at the wall. The projector should not be placed at an angle, or the sides of the image will not be equal and the corners will not be square. Measure the top, bottom, and both sides of the projected image, to make sure that the machine points straight at the wall.

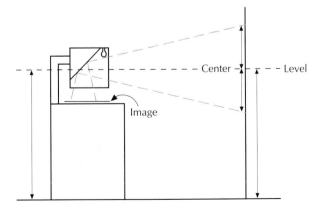

Using a Slide Projector

Another way to enlarge an image is to project a slide of it onto a wall. Similar limitations that apply to the use of an opaque projector apply to this method of enlargement. It usually won't work well for making finished designs with dimensions larger than four or five feet. The farther you move the projector from the projection wall, the larger and dimmer the image will be. When placing the projector, follow the instructions given for using the opaque projector to make sure it is pointing straight at the wall.

Using a Grid

Many artists use grids to enlarge their designs. In this method, a grid is drawn over the original design and a larger-scale grid is drawn over the cartoon.

Place or tape a piece of tracing paper, clear mylar, or drafting acetate over the original image. Draw a horizontal line 1" below the top edge of the design. Draw lines parallel to this first line, spaced 1" apart. Draw a vertical line 1" from the left edge of the design. Make sure it is perpendicular to the horizontal lines you just drew. Draw lines, 1" apart, parallel to this first line, working across the design to make the grid.

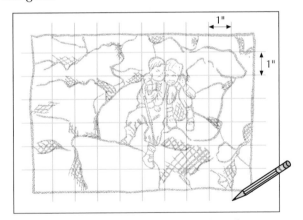

On the paper for the cartoon, draw lines representing the edges of the quilt. Draw horizontal lines from top to bottom in this space. The distance between these lines is determined by the scale factor you used when you decided on the finished dimensions of the quilt. If the scale factor is $5\frac{1}{2}$, draw the lines $5\frac{1}{2}$" apart. Draw vertical lines across the cartoon. Use the same scale factor for the distance separating these lines, or 5½" for the example below. One square inch on the original image equals one square on the grid.

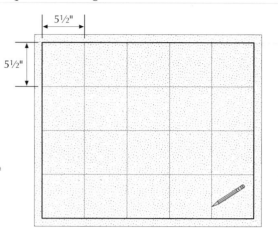

Obtain greater accuracy by using finer grids. Try drawing a grid using ½" squares instead of 1" squares on the original image. Of course, you must then remember to draw additional lines halfway between the original lines (2¾" for our example) when you draw the cartoon. For even finer grids, try gridded tracing paper, available in 4, 8, and 10 squares to the inch.

If your image is already in the form of a sketch, you're a step ahead here. Work in pencil. Choose a line in the sketch. Find the first grid line that it crosses. Put a small mark on the cartoon in approximately the same place on the corresponding grid line. Place marks on all the grid lines that the sketch line crosses. Sketch the line on the cartoon, using these marks as a guide. For smooth lines, try using a flexible curve to connect the marks.

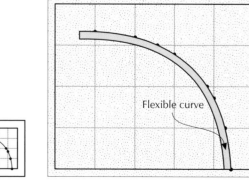

Original image   Cartoon

Step back and look at the two sketches from several feet away. Make any necessary adjustments. Because you are working on a foundation, the line doesn't have to be exactly the same as the image. The pattern pieces will still fit together. Continue to transfer sketch lines until they are all transferred, and the cartoon is complete.

If you are working from a photo, the process is a little different. Discrete lines are seldom present in photos so you must create them. I recommend using felt-tip markers or crayons to color the areas in each square on the cartoon to match the photo. Color less important areas sketchily and pay more attention to detail in the important areas.

Once the image is transferred to the cartoon, you are ready for the next translation stage: adding composition lines to enhance the design.

DRAWING COMPOSITION LINES

Work in pencil. Draw the highest-contrast, most important lines first; make these the main composition lines. Then decide where you want to lay down seams to delineate detail in the image. In a seascape, this could be wave crests, eddies in the water, or color shifts. These lines do not have to form continuous seam lines; they can stop in the middle of an area. However, they should mark visual changes in the image.

Decide where you want to add lines to facilitate shading and texturing of the image. These could be lines echoing other lines, or they could be crosshatched or gridded lines. They could be delineated by polygonal networking. They do not have to be seam lines but can be lines added to increase the viewer's sense of shape or depth.

Eliminate, alter, or add elements as you fancy. Play!

If a line bothers you, step back and try to visualize how it would look better. Sketch it several times in different ways. Pin blank paper over problem areas and sketch alternate ideas to audition them. Which one do you like best?

DRAWING THE SEAM LINES

This is the next translation stage. Continue to work in pencil. Step back from the design you have developed so far. In the designing stage, change anything that bothers you about the work. If you don't like a line, stop and ask yourself where it should be, or if it should be there at all. Use an eraser gently.

If you feel some of the design is working, draw a heavy, dark pencil line over it. Translate "design lines" into "seam lines." Are these lines seams that you can piece? If they are not, can you add seams to ease construction, such as a seam off of a leaf point? Remember that seams completely surround pattern pieces. They cannot stop in the middle of a piece; they must connect to another seam or at the edge of the quilt.

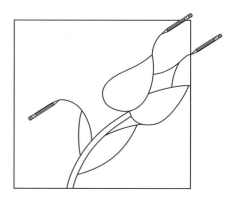

Add seams to ease construction.

If the seams are too difficult to piece, can they be modified? Simplified? Unified?

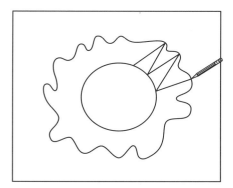

Continue to play with the lines until you feel you have good seams for piecing your design. Add more seams to ease construction as necessary. Remember that two identical fabrics sewn together form an almost invisible seam. Such seams don't affect the composition but can greatly aid construction. Check to see that every piece of the quilt has a seam around its entire edge.

If the contrast across a line shifts so that the line seems to disappear, break up the area with many small seams and incorporate shading into the area. This is a good spot to use string or polygonal piecing.

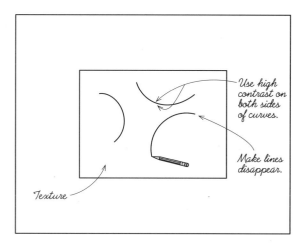

Use high contrast on both sides of curves.

Make lines disappear.

Texture

Sketch with Design Lines

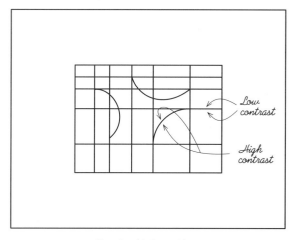

Low contrast

High contrast

Sketch with Seam Lines

Check the design once again to see if it needs any more adjustments. When you are satisfied with the pencil drawing, draw over the seam lines using ink. If you change your mind after the lines are drawn in ink, remove them with white-out and redraw.

At each step in this process, you can get a better feel for the image by looking at it through a camera. This reduces the image so that individual details become unimportant and you can focus on the overall design.

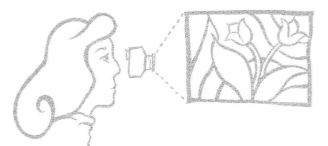

DESIGNING THE BORDER

The border of the quilt is an intrinsic part of the design. There are as many possibilities for the border as for the design itself.

Traditionally, the border for a quilt was treated as a visual frame, with borders often added as afterthoughts and with piecing kept to a minimum. The binding and borders of working bed quilts take the brunt of the wear and tear, so spending long hours designing and working on a border may not have been worth the extra effort for utilitarian quilts.

With the advent of wall quilts, more attention has been focused on borders, with more elaborately pieced borders appearing. Appliqué and embellishment enliven plain borders. On some quilts, the border dominates the design.

Regardless of the approach you take in designing your border, consider the following.

Keep the border balanced with the rest of the design. An effective border enhances the center area by working with it as a cohesive unit. It doesn't distract the viewer from the center or compete with it. A successful border keeps the viewer's eye from wandering away from the quilt, stopping the action of the design at the outer edge and bringing the eye back to the center. The border used as a frame emphasizes the design.

You can design pieced borders and inner borders easily into the original cartoon. The illustration below shows how a pieced border extends the design to the edges of the quilt and how an inner border provides a visual break in the design.

In "I'm Going to Eat You Little Fisheys" on page 8, I used the kelp to visually border the fish. Borders may be anything from simple strips of rotary-cut fabric strips to complex foundation piecing. They do not need to be square, straight, or symmetrical.

CHOOSING FABRICS

The fabrics chosen for a quilt greatly affect the design. Fabric choice is the final major translation from sketch to quilt. I prefer to begin with a palette of fabrics before I start the design process, and these fabrics often act as a source of inspiration to me. The fabrics themselves suggest a design. Sometimes I think the quilt is already in the fabric, and I merely remove the unneeded bits to expose it.

In many ways, the fabric selection is more important than the seams. If a seam line is a little awkward, few will notice, but an awkward fabric choice can kill a good quilt.

Fabric colors play an important role in quilts. If you feel shy about color choice, I suggest that you visit your quilt shop or bookstore to find excellent books on color. Many quilt and fabric shops, community colleges, and art- and craft-supply stores offer classes on color. My advice regarding color choice is to use what you like and go with your instincts. It's your money, time, sweat, design, and quilt. Do what pleases you.

IDENTIFYING PROBLEMS

Sometimes you may have a distinct feeling that there is something indefinable wrong with your design. Or you may just get stuck and not know how to continue.

Creative block can be a real problem. Do not give up. There are some tricks that might help.

❧ Turn the design upside down or on its side. Sometimes inverting or rotating an image gives you the change in perspective that you need to see what's wrong.

❧ Put the piece away for a while or work on something else. Allowing some time and clearing your mind may help you take a fresh look at the work later.

❧ Display the design so that it's the first thing you see in the morning. Sometimes your first impression is your best.

❧ Make yourself work on the project for thirty minutes each day. Sometimes you get bogged down on a project and need to work on it in short but regular intervals to get back into it.

❧ Ask for help from a friend or person you know. Ask people who don't work in fabric. They don't carry around the same preconceptions and conditioning that quilters do. (Of course, they may not understand either!)

❧ Crop the image. Take strips of neutral material, such as black paper, and use them to block off areas of the image, usually along the edges. Sometimes you only need to recenter or remove parts of the design.

PROJECT:
KATHLEEN
O'HANLON'S
QUILT

54" x 46"

Kathleen O'Hanlon created this quilt for a friend. Enlarge the gridded sketch above to make a full-size cartoon and follow the basic guidelines below for assembling the quilt.

ASSEMBLY

1. Draw a full-size cartoon from the gridded sketch above. For enlarging a design using a grid, see pages 95–96. Prepare a freezer-paper pattern. (See "Making the Pattern" on page 17.)

2. For sections 1–9, count the squares in the illustration and cut enough 2½" x 2½" squares for each section. Arrange and sew together. Using the pattern you made in step 1 and referring to the lines in the illustration below, trim

each section to the correct shape. Make sure piece 6's V notch lies on a seam.

3. String-piece web sections and arcs 10–46. See "String Piecing" on pages 34–41.

4. Assemble webs and sections 1–9, following the diagram below for joining the final seams. See "Simple Piecing" on pages 16–23.

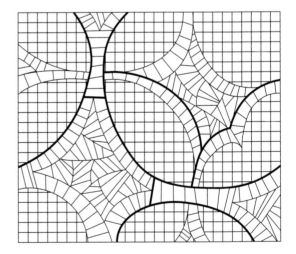

5. Add 1"-wide inner borders and 3½"-wide outer borders. Trace around a saucer or bowl as a pattern for rounded corners.

6. Layer the quilt top with batting and backing; baste and quilt as desired. Bind the edges. (Kathleen used a stitch-and-turn binding for her quilt. See pages 108–9.)

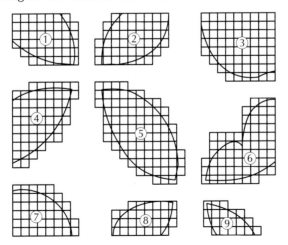

Untitled by Kathleen O'Hanlon, 1993, Seattle, Washington, 54" x 46". Soft pinks and turquoises contribute webs of color to this abstract design. Collection of Teresa Posakony.

This section discusses the steps necessary to complete a quilt from a pieced top. It is for those persistent souls who believe in the contemplation, at least, of finishing a project—I salute you! Without you, there would be no quilt shows!

The basics of bordering, marking, basting, quilting, and binding a quilt are covered in this section. For more detailed explanations of these steps, books from The Joy of Quilting series (That Patchwork Place) are excellent quiltmaking resources. Check your local quilt shop, bookstore, or library for more books written specifically on these topics.

FINDING A WORK AREA

For squaring a quilt, the best work area is large enough to lay the work out flat with room for you to move around all four sides. The best work surface is a non-slip surface that can withstand the heat of being ironed. Ideally, we'd all have a studio with a huge table covered in layers of newspaper and topped with stretched canvas to work on.

A suitable alternative is to shove all the furniture in your living room (or someone else's living room) to the walls so you can work on the carpet.

Some carpets burn or melt easily (test a small area in an out-of-the-way place first), so spread sheets, old bedspreads, or fabric over them. Spread the protective layers out so they lie smooth. Stick T pins through the layers, into the carpet, to hold them in place.

If nothing else is available, try using folding tables. Slide them together to create a work space large enough for your quilt.

CHECKING THE QUILT TOP

Spread out the unquilted top, right side up. Stand back and really look at it. Now is the time to catch those little errors that haunt you later. Does any stay stitching show on the front? Are there any seams you'd like to fix or points that don't align?

Starting from the center and working toward the edges, press the entire top. As you press, try to ease any fullness out to the edges. At this stage, it is more important that the top lies flat than that it is square.

If it won't lie flat, now is the time to fix it. Lay the original cartoon over the work. Find the longest continuous or most prominent seam, or the element of the design that is most important. Stick at least two pins straight down through the cartoon seam and into the same place on the work to anchor the cartoon.

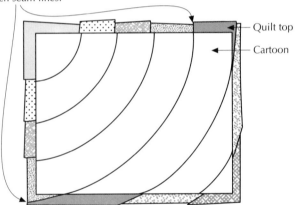

Match seam lines.

Quilt top

Cartoon

Compare the cartoon seams to the seams at the edges of the quilt. Where do they fall out of alignment? Does the error begin in one place and slowly accumulate? Is one particular seam the culprit? Correct the seams until the work lies flat.

SQUARING THE QUILT

Squaring is a process of trimming the edge of the work to the shape of its original design.

This process helps correct accumulated errors

and is similar to squaring blocks before setting them. It can be done both before adding a border and after the quilting is completed. The instructions below are the same for squaring a quilt top or a quilted quilt. To make the section clearer, I will refer to them both as the quilt.

If the design is meant to be square or rectangular, place T pins at each corner. Make sure that the pins penetrate through the work into the work surface behind. Using a metal measuring tape or ruler, measure the distance between the corner pins at the top and the pins at the bottom. The distance should be the same. If it isn't, move the pins on the longer side until they are the same distance apart at the top and bottom.

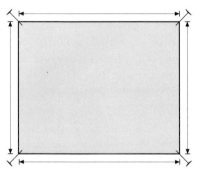

Measure the distance between the pins diagonally across the work. The diagonals should be the same length. If they aren't, move both of the pins on the long diagonal to shorten it.

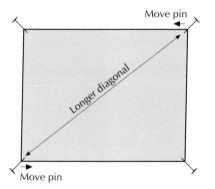

Recheck all the measurements and adjust the pins until the sides and the diagonals agree. Wind a thread around one of the pins. Wind it around the pin at the adjacent corner, continuing around all four pins until the thread stretches snugly around the edge of the quilt.

The thread should be snug but not tight enough to pull the pins out.

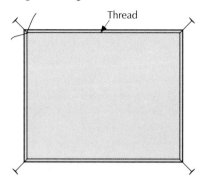

These threads mark straight lines parallel to the edges of the quilt. Working on one side at a time, slide a long straight edge up to the edge of the quilt. (A clear plastic quilt ruler works very well.) If the quilt extends to the thread along the entire side, mark or trim the edge right under the thread.

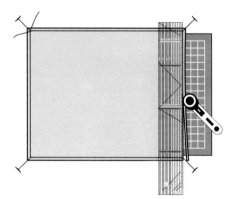

If there is a gap between the quilt and the thread, mark or trim the entire side of the quilt an equal distance inside the thread.

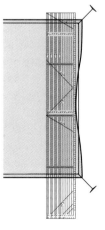

Note: If you are concerned about bias edges along the edges of the quilt, carefully staystitch $1/4$" to $1/2$" along the edges of the quilt. Stabilize the fabric by basting carefully, quilting closely, and using a single, unseamed backing fabric.

MARKING QUILTING LINES

When you are designing your quilting pattern, consider how much time and thought you put into designing the piecing of the quilt. The quilting deserves at least as much thought.

Use the same design techniques for both processes. Try making sketches first on paper, then use chalk to test designs—it can be removed if you don't like the effect. As you would carefully design the borders of the quilt, choose the quilting pattern to enhance and work with the quilt's piecing design.

PREPARING THE BACKING

For the quilt backing, choose a pieced design or make it from a single fabric. If it is pieced, prepare it as if it were a quilt top. Make the backing at least 2" larger than the top so that it extends at least 1" beyond the top on all sides. Fold the backing in half lengthwise and mark or pin the fold at each end. Unfold the backing and spread it out flat, wrong side up. Press.

BASTING

Basting is an under-appreciated art. It's hard on the back and fingers, tedious, and uncreative. It is, however, necessary. Poor or insufficient basting is one of the major causes of problems in quilts.

Whether you baste with thread or safety pins, the best rule is to baste until you just can't stand to baste anymore. If you plan to hand quilt on a frame, less basting is required since the layers don't have as much opportunity to shift. For lap or machine quilting, the heavier the basting, the better.

Tape the backing down with masking tape, stretching it out a little to avoid tucks in the back of the quilt. Center the batting over the backing and spread it out. Spread the center portion of the top, right side up, over the batting.

Make sure that the batting and the backing extend at least 1" beyond the edge of the top all around, then press the top from the center out to spread it out. This helps to knit the three layers together. Set the iron to the lowest temperature required for the fibers you are using. If you are using polyester batting with a cotton top, use a polyester setting. Now you are ready to baste.

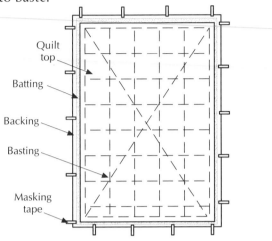

Quilt top

Batting

Backing

Basting

Masking tape

Baste a cotton quilt every 4" to 5" or more. It's best to baste a silk quilt every 2" to 3". Baste from the quilt's center toward the edges and work systematically across the quilt.

If you do not have a work surface large enough for the entire piece, line up the center portion of the backing with one edge of the work surface and spread out as much of it as you can.

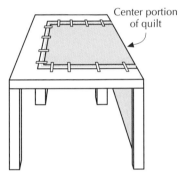

Center portion of quilt

Baste the quilt in sections, complete one section, remove the tape, and begin again with the next section. Make sure to smooth out the layers as you change sections so you won't have wrinkles between sections.

When basting, hold a spoon in the opposite hand to scoop up the point of the needle or the safety pin. Try wearing a rubber secretarial fingertip to grab the needle more easily when pulling it through the fabric. This is a good way to reduce fatigue.

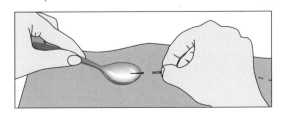

QUILTING When deciding whether to quilt by machine or by hand, weigh the advantages and disadvantages as they relate to your project. The more seams there are, the harder hand quilting becomes. This is particularly true in polygonal piecing, where six or eight seams frequently come together at one point.

Hand quilting

Machine quilting

The most common hand quilting stitch is the running stitch. Make the running stitch by pushing the tip of the needle through the quilt and just out the back. Rotate the needle and push it so that it comes back up and out the top of the quilt. This is done most easily with the middle finger or the thumb.

Wear a thimble on the pushing finger to protect it. Some quilters wear a thimble on both hands, with the thimble on the hand under the quilt worn to protect the finger or to hold the quilt up when returning the needle to the top.

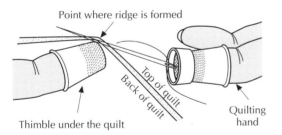

Point where ridge is formed

Top of quilt
Back of quilt

Thimble under the quilt

Quilting hand

Most quilters find thimbles helpful for quilting. Thimbles come in different sizes. Make sure to use a properly fitting thimble. Most aren't made to fit well over long fingernails, although there are thimbles available in quilt shops or mail-order catalogs that do accommodate long fingernails. Nonmetallic (plastic and leather) thimbles and finger protectors are also available.

A tailor's thimble, a rare kind of thimble

used in England, is worn on the thumb. It is open on the end, and the pushing is done with the side of the thimble. These can be hard to find, but they are invaluable. By wearing the thimble on either the middle finger or the thumb, you can sew in any direction with the same hand.

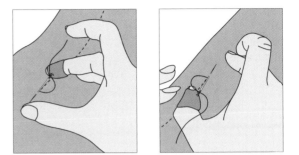

If you choose to machine quilt, be sure to bring the thread ends to the front of the quilt, knot them, thread them through a large-eyed needle, and bury them inside the quilt.

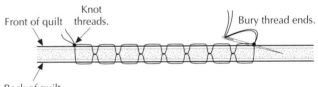

Knot threads.
Front of quilt
Bury thread ends.
Back of quilt

SQUARING THE QUILTED QUILT

Before the binding is pinned in place, square the quilt again. A quilted quilt, in contrast to a quilt top, is three-dimensional—it has thickness. A line of quilting, sewn through all three layers, distorts the quilt. The quilt "pulls or draws up," becoming smaller. Irregular areas or amounts of quilting cause the quilt to draw up more in some directions than others. Squaring the quilt evens up some of this distortion and helps keep the edge of the quilt from rippling.

Square the quilted quilt exactly the same way as you would an unquilted top. Follow the instructions for "Squaring the Quilt" on pages 102–3. After squaring the quilt, but before moving it, pin the binding in place.

BINDING

There are many types of binding, from purchased double-fold bias tape to handmade piping or fringe. They all serve the same purpose: to finish the edge. The instructions below are for facing, single fold, French or double fold, and stitch-and-turn binding. For other binding techniques, see *Happy Endings* by Mimi Dietrich (That Patchwork Place).

Facing Method

Use this method for quilts with straight or irregular edges. It does not show on the front of the quilt but is turned entirely to the back like a collar facing. It is an excellent binding to use with scalloped edges.

1. Cut 2"-wide (or wider) strips of binding fabric. Cut these strips either across the width of the fabric or on the bias. (Quilts with irregular edges must be bound with bias binding or the binding must be trimmed to match the shape.)

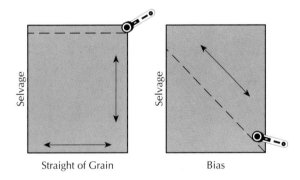

Straight of Grain   Bias

2. If the binding strips are cut on grain, trim the ends square. If they are cut on the bias, trim the ends of the strips at a 45° angle.

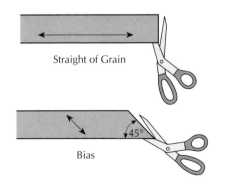

Straight of Grain

Bias

3. Join the strips by sewing them end to end, right sides together, with ¼"-wide seam allowances. Sew strips together to make a binding strip long enough to sew all the way around the quilt. Press the seam allowances open.

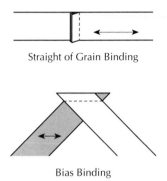

Straight of Grain Binding

Bias Binding

4. Pin the binding, right sides together, all around the edge of the quilt. Start in the middle of the bottom of the quilt. When you reach the first corner, clip the seam allowance of the binding ¼" to allow for ease.

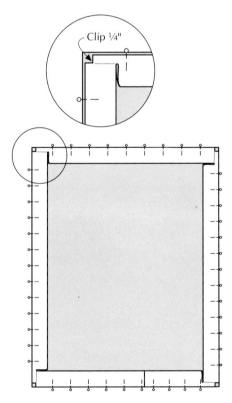

Clip ¼"

5. Pin the binding down the next side. Smooth the binding flat between pins, but do not pull it to create tension. When you reach the beginning of the binding, overlap the two ends and fold back the end that lies underneath to make a ¼"-wide seam. Pin and blindstitch this seam later when sewing the binding to the back of the quilt.

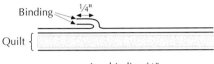

Lap binding ¼".

6. Sew the binding to the quilt with a ½"-wide seam all the way around the edge of the quilt, through the binding and the quilt. Clip the corners to reduce the bulk.

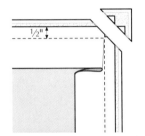

7. From the back, trim the backing and batting to within ⅛" from stitching to reduce bulk. Do not trim the top.

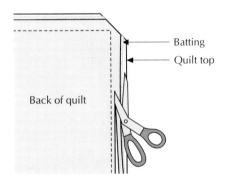

8. With the quilt laid out flat, turn the binding to the back of the quilt. Pin in place next to the edge.

9. Turn the edge of the binding under ½" and pin in place. Fold the binding in a miter at the corners. Stitch down with a hem or blind stitch. Be sure to sew up the opening in the mi-

tered corners and the seam where the ends of the binding overlap.

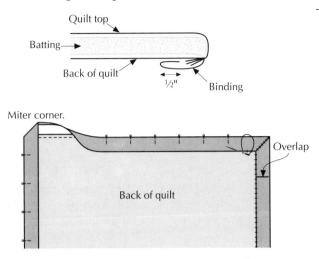

Miter corner.

Single-Fold Binding

This binding is meant to show on the front of the quilt and adds to the overall design. I like to make my own extra-wide binding and piece it from different fabrics. Consider using jazzy prints, stripes, or contrasting fabrics.

1. For a standard ½"-wide finished single-fold binding, cut strips of the binding fabric 2" wide. (See steps 1 and 2 for "Facing Method" on page 106.)

2. Sew the strips together end to end, placing them right sides together and joining them with ½"-wide seams. Sew strips together to make a binding strip long enough to sew all the way around the edge of the quilt. Press the seam allowances open.

3. Pin the binding, right sides together, around the edge of the quilt. Begin in the middle of the lower edge of the quilt. When you reach the corner, fold the binding over at a 45° angle and then down along the next side.

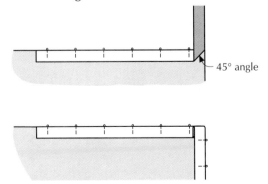

4. When you reach the beginning of the binding, fold the beginning over ¹/₂" and overlap the end of the strip. Join binding ends and trim. Sew binding in place with a ¹/₂"-wide seam all the way around the quilt.

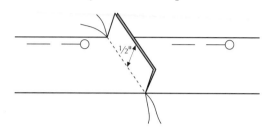

5. Turn the binding over the edge of the quilt. On the back of the quilt, fold the raw edge of the binding under ¹/₂" and hem in place with a blind or hem stitch. Sew the opening in the mitered corners and the seam where the ends of the binding overlap.

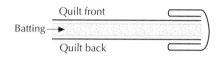

French or Double-Fold Binding

French or double-fold binding is favored by many quilters for the strong, firm edge it gives to the quilt.

1. Following the directions for cutting binding strips on page 106, cut 2"-wide binding strips.
2. Cut the ends of each strip at a 45° angle and join. (See step 3 for joining bias ends on page 106.)
3. Fold and press the binding in half lengthwise, with wrong sides together. Fold one end of the binding under at a 45° angle as shown.

4. Pin the binding to the front of the quilt. Starting 3" from the beginning of the binding and using a ¹/₄"-wide seam allowance, stitch. Continue stitching, stopping within ¹/₄" of the end. Remove from the machine. Fold binding up to make a 45°-angle fold as shown, then fold the binding back down along the next edge. Begin stitching from the edge of the quilt

and repeat for all four sides of the quilt. Stop stitching within 3" from the beginning.

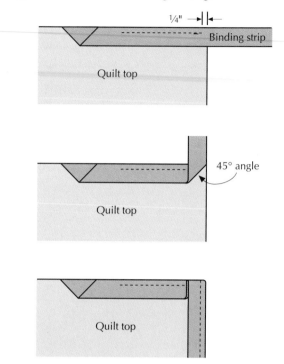

5. Tuck the end of the binding into the beginning, then finish sewing the binding to the quilt.

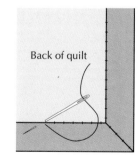

6. Fold the binding over to the back of the quilt and blindstitch to the backing along the fold of the binding. At each corner, sew the opening in the miter.

Stitch-and-Turn

This is the only binding technique in which the edge of the quilt is finished before the quilt is quilted. The quilt, batting, and backing are sewn together, then turned, much like you would make a pillow. No actual binding is involved, and no binding shows on the front of the quilt. This is an excellent method to use with irregularly shaped quilts.

1. Lay the batting on the work surface and place the quilt top over the batting, right side up. Lay the backing over the quilt top with right sides together. Very carefully, pin around all of the edges, placing pins every 2" or less. If the layers shift during stitching, the quilt will not lie flat.

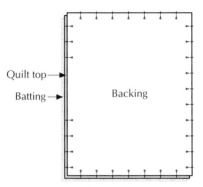

2. Sew a $\frac{1}{4}$"-wide seam all the way around the edge, leaving a 4"- to 5"-long opening. (For very large quilts, make the opening larger.) Remove the pins and trim only the batting to within $\frac{1}{8}$" from the seam.

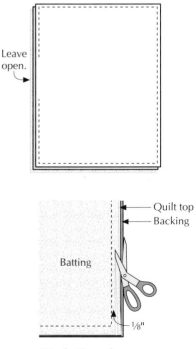

Trim batting only.

3. Turn the quilt right sides out and close the opening by hand with a blind or whip stitch.

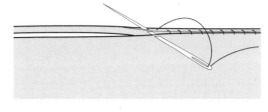

4. Press the edges to turn them crisply, then baste the quilt. (See "Basting" on page 104.) Quilt as desired.

LABELING AND SIGNING

After all the work you've put into your quilt, be sure to label it. Choose from a variety of permanent marking pens suitable for fabric. Typewriter ink is permanent and is used by many quilters to document their quilts. Other possibilities include embroidery and fabric paints.

On a swatch of fabric, record your name, the date the quilt was finished, your address, the title of the quilt, its dimensions, and anything else you want to include. Write a poem or message along with the quilt recipient's name. Write a few words about the inspiration for the design.

Labels don't have to be plain white cotton. They can be original documentations, pieced and embellished.

SHOWING AND SHARING

The last and most delightful step is to share your work with others. You deserve it. Whether you just put the quilt on the bed for others to see, take it for sharing to your quilt group, hang it in a show, or give it to someone, share it! The more you show it, the more joy it'll give.

Tea Garden

Directions start on page 44.

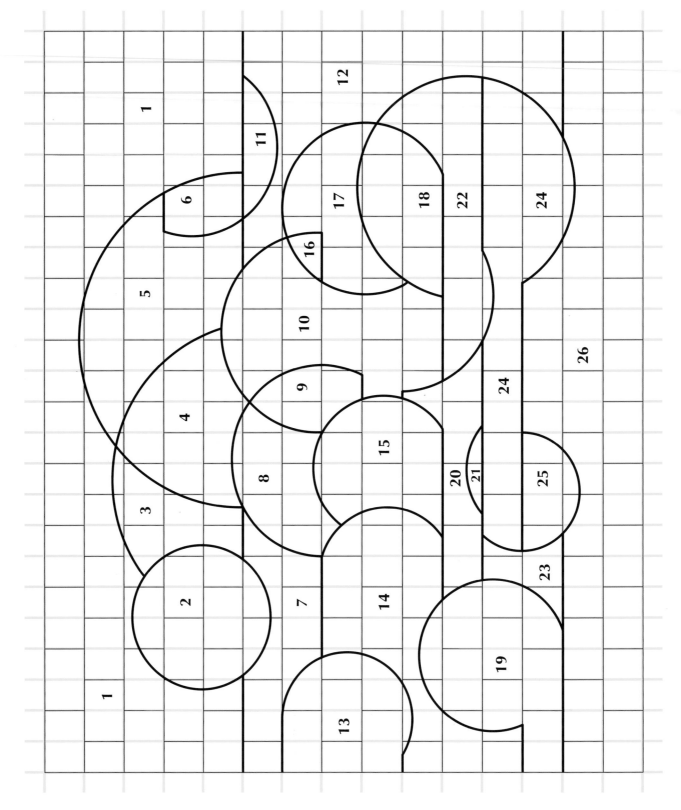

Otto

Directions start on page 56.

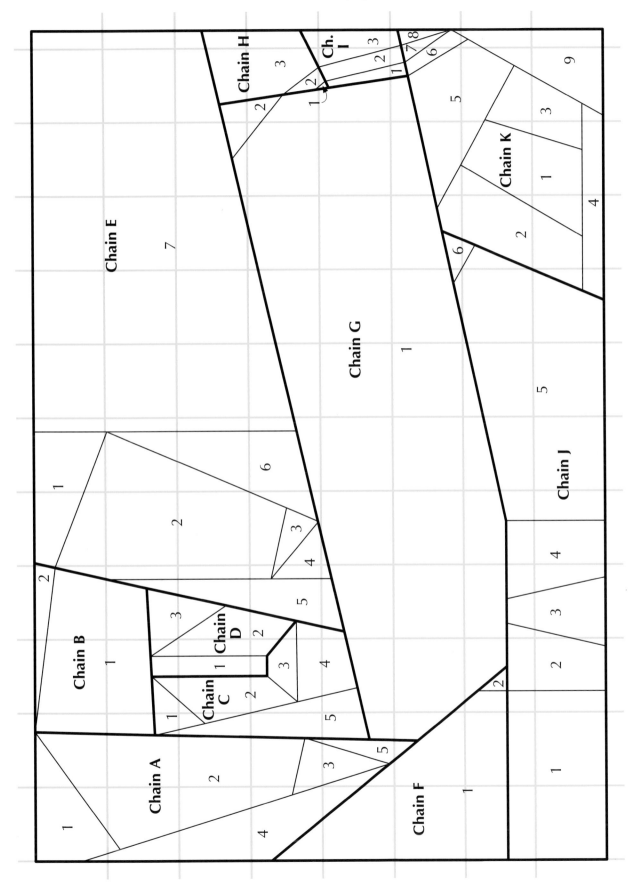

For me, art and craft are tightly interwoven. I come from a strong heritage of fine craftsmen and women who worked in practical, tactile media and whose creations do not meet the academic definition of "Art." For us, the process has always been as important as the product. Our rewards are personal and private. Individual development is a personal journey.

I strongly believe that the creative impulse is as inherent in humans as the need to breathe or sleep. We are the most open to this impulse as children when the world is still full of wonder for us. We may create in mud pies, music, marbles, or words. We may create with food or computer bits. We may turn just cleaning a room, planting a field, or caring for the elderly into a confirmation of life and creativity. Each of us finds our own medium. But we do create.

As we grow up, we tend to absorb cultural ideas that may inhibit our responses to this impulse. We are taught arbitrary definitions for "art" and "artists." Still more destructively, we are taught how to judge art and artistic talent. Much of our journey as adult artists is to unlearn this unnecessary baggage.

Ultimately, each of us is responsible for our own journey. Formal art training is available, but it is not the only way to learn. Just as we cannot really learn a language without using it, we cannot grow as artists without creating. If you want to grow, push your limits. Try new things. Avoid judging your work or comparing it to others' work. They have their own path and this should be your own journey.

MEET THE AUTHOR

Mia Rozmyn has been a fiber artist since 1969. She gave up weaving, spinning, and natural dyeing for quilting and dye painting in 1989. She has a bachelor's degree in civil engineering from the University of Washington and worked at The Boeing Company until she and her husband decided to start a family.

Mia now lives with her husband, two sons, a dog, and a cat in Seattle. She has "a little problem" with fabric—she lives three blocks from In The Beginning, one of the largest quilt shops in the area.

For her quilts, Mia works primarily with silk and cotton. Her work has been seen in international shows as well as numerous local shows. Mia currently teaches quilting in many locales, including her own region, Western Washington.